CROSS CULTURAL COMMUNICATION

CROSS CULTURAL COMMUNICATION

BY

NICHOLAS DIMA PH.D.

INSTITUTE FOR THE STUDY OF MAN
1133 13th Street, N.W., Suite C-2
Washington, D.C. 20005

© Copyright, Nicholas Dima 1990

Library of Congress Catalog Card Number:

ISBN 0-941694-36-4

Contents

INTRODUCTION 7

CHAPTER 1
   MAN, CULTURE, SOCIETY AND COMMUNICATION 15

CHAPTER 2
   TECHNOLOGICAL PROGRESS, CULTURAL CHANGE,
   AND COMMUNICATION 33

CHAPTER 3
   PERSONALITY FORMATION AND COMMUNICATION 47

CHAPTER 4
   THE AMERICAN MODAL PERSONALITY 57

CHAPTER 5
   CULTURE SHOCK AND CULTURAL ADJUSTMENT 65

CHAPTER 6
   VERBAL AND NONVERBAL COMMUNICATION 71

CHAPTER 7
   ENGLISH AS AN INTERNATIONAL LANGUAGE 85

CHAPTER 8
   POLITICAL CULTURE AND COMMUNICATION 93

CHAPTER 9
   THE WORLD'S RELIGIONS 105

CHAPTER 10
   CONCLUDING REMARKS 119

BIBLIOGRAPHY 127

Introduction

I experienced my first real culture shock when I was about nineteen. For the first and only time in my native Romania, I was allowed to go to neighboring Bulgaria to participate in a youth swimming and water polo competition. Everyone on our team was amazed to see Bulgarians shaking their heads right and left to express their nonverbal sign for *yes*, and nodding them up and down for no. First, we thought that it was all a joke, but then we realized they were serious, and we were puzzled. Having lived in isolation like ourselves, the Bulgarians were also deeply surprised. We made fun of them and they made fun of us. The strange thing, however, came after a few days of fun and laughter when we no longer knew who was "right" and who was "wrong."

A few months later I decided that I had had enough of Marxist ideology and tried to escape to the West. Young and inexperienced, I was caught at the Yugoslav border and spent the next four years in Communist prison and labor camps. It turned out to be the most shocking but richest experience of my lifetime, and I have never stopped wondering at the diversity and complexity of life everywhere.

When I managed to eventually escape and come to the United States, I was again completely disoriented and, in many ways, had to relearn everything from scratch. During my first week in America I found a job. When finishing work in the early afternoon, I could not believe that people greeted each other "good night." Good night in the middle of the afternoon with the sun still up in the skies? These Americans are strange!

In the beginning, I blamed my confusion on my poor English and immediately embarked on an all-out effort to master the new language. I eventually learned it, but the problems of misunderstanding and miscommunication did not cease. It was then that I concluded the Bible was wrong, at least in one respect. When the people of Babylon decided to build the Babel Tower to reach for the heavens, God allegedly confounded their languages so that they would no longer understand each other and would not be able to erect the tower. I believe, however, that God confounded their minds. How else can one explain that we often speak the same language, but only understand what we already have in our minds?

There are numerous examples of confusion resulting from the meaning, connotation, and importance we attach to various words and expressions even when we use the same language. While visiting France, for example, an American couple went to a restaurant for dinner and the lady asked for a diet coke. Puzzled, the waiter retorted defensively, "Mme. this is a restaurant, not a hospital." Every traveler notices and expects environmental differences from country to country and from region to region. But we continue to be surprised with the great variety of cultures and human behavior in the world.

While in Kathmandu, I bought a "tangka," which is a painting typical of Nepal, usually depicting a religious or philosophical theme. Knowing something about the Oriental propensity to haggle, I managed to bring the price down from over $100 to about $70. Back in the States I went to a frame shop and was glad to see that the frame was only $30. Then, however, I had the haggling in reverse. "Do you want glass, too?" "Of course I want it, what is a frame without glass?" "This is $6 in addition." "Do you want non-glare glass? This is $3 extra." "Do you want the painting to be flattened first?" At this point I simply stared at the frame salesman, but he continued: "Do you want it framed, or you will do the framing yourself? There is the sales tax too." In the end the frame cost me almost as much as the painting. And I wondered "who are the better businessmen, the haggling Orientals or the cool Americans?"

If one manages to extricate himself from the culture which has produced him, he or she would be extremely surprised to see how different the same world appears to be from another perspective. One cannot dare offer beef to a Hindu or pork to a Moslem or an Orthodox Jew. Yet some people in the Far East butcher dogs and consider their meat a delicacy. The same dogs are considered impure and not even touched by most Moslems, are badly mistreated and abused by people in many countries, are kept as a strict necessity in most of Africa, are respected as a unique form of life in India, and are treated almost as members of the family by many Americans.

Politics, ideology, and religion, which influence our behavior continuously and touch our lives on a daily basis, are among the most delicate subjects to discuss not only cross-culturally, but also within the same culture as well. Some of the ideological contradictions are so grave that one wonders, how can we hope to build new bridges and avoid more bloody confrontations in the future?

During the last decade, new forms of religious ferment took the world by surprise. "America is worse than Britain; Britain is worse than America. The Soviet Union is worse than both of them," declared Ayatollah Khomeini. Unfortunately, he expressed the feelings and frustrations of a growing number of moslems, and Islam has become indeed a major ideological force in the present world. Colonel Qadhafi, for example, gave the following view of the Palestinians and Israelis in an interview printed in *US News and World Report* on November 6, 1986.

Q: What is the resolution of the Palestinian question?
A: There is no resolution. The Palestinian people, behind the Arab

nation, will continue fighting till the end.

Q: Is the end the destruction of Israel? Is that the final solution?
A: Maybe the destruction of the Arabs, maybe the destruction of Israel.

Qadhafi may be an aberrant player in the contemporary power politics, but the ongoing struggle of the Palestinians remains an issue of cultural and political misunderstanding. And what not so long ago was a faraway place with its own problems is now everybody's concern. Misunderstanding and lack of communication in the present world can jeopardize the entire civilization of man.

Each man is in many ways a unique creature. He not only has his own signature at his fingertips and a genetic formula exclusively his own, but also every man has unique experiences, perceptions, and assumptions with which he communicates and works with others. During our evolution from the stone age to the space age, human societies have moved from small and isolated groups to the present global world. In the process, man has learned to compromise and live with each other, and is still learning. The beauty of the present world is such that people live at various levels of interaction, communication, and awareness – from a few remaining tribal societies to those who probe the edge of the known universe and plan the colonization of space.

There are currently over 160 independent countries in the world, hundreds of major ethnic groups, an even greater diversity of cultures, and at least 3,000 spoken languages. At the same time, immediate communication virtually everywhere, rapid transportation, global trade, worldwide political interaction, and universal interdependence are ever growing and expanding. Understanding each other and communicating across linguistic, political, religious, and other cultural barriers have become a "must" in today's world if we are to succeed. It has been estimated that as of 1987, there were about 10,000 Japanese business executives in the United States, virtually all of whom spoke English and had a good understanding of American culture. At the same time, there were only some 1,000 American executives in Japan, only a handful of whom spoke Japanese. Knowing the poor performance of US businesses in Japan, one can only wonder how many of those American executives had a good grasp of Japanese culture and business behavior?

The post-war geopolitical reality has made America a unique country in the world, with equally unique privileges and responsibilities. For many years, the United States was unchallenged economically, politically, and militarily, but the balance of power has changed. From a military point of view, the Soviet Union remains an enemy of the Western World. It is also a more powerful rival than ever before, although allegedly Moscow is now willing to negotiate and compromise.

Economically the world has changed dramatically as well. Some of our best friends – for example, Japan and West Germany – have become some of our fiercest competitors. The Third World has also become a force to reckon with, and important geographic regions, such as Eastern Europe, the Middle East, and Central America, require a permanent effort of understanding and an adjustment of policies.

American businessmen, students, diplomats, and military men are now involved with other countries virtually all over the world. Their success depends to a large degree on their understanding of these cultures, on their knowledge of American interests and obligations in the area, and on their own communication skills. An equally important factor often ignored is a good understanding of American culture. We tend to take our own culture and values for granted. Most of the time we judge others by our own values system: by what we believe is right or wrong, good or bad, normal or deviant, and so on. The truth is that such basic values may differ from society to society, and we become aware of our culture only when separated from it, finding ourselves in a strange environment. Only when we are confronted with another culture do we develop a better understanding of our own, and possibly of others.

We should be able to identify some of the most important American cultural traits, the great achievements and contributions of the United States to the civilization of the world, and some of the weaknesses of American society. While I do not recommend quick self-criticism, I would stress that knowing your weaknesses makes you stronger in many situations.

Last, but not least. If this manual is to be used by governmental representatives, it should be stressed from the start that all US officials are assigned abroad to PERFORM a specific function for a precise PURPOSE and for a specified DURATION. This is a particular case of cross-cultural communication. They must always remember that they work for the US government. Consequently, they may sympathize with the local people and interests, but they must not GO NATIVE. Actually, this is neither possible nor desirable. Occasionally, they may even have to recommend or implement policies contrary to their personal principles and beliefs. This is a particular case of cross-cultural communication, which in a way, is simple because of its limitations, yet difficult because of its restrictions.

Understanding well their position between the US government and the authorities of a given country, as well as knowing basic American values and those of the people where they are assigned, is only half the problem. The other half is bridging them, and this involves further knowledge of "man," "culture," and "societies."

One can be shocked seeing how diverse cultures are in various parts of the world, but be equally surprised at how similar human beings are. Everywhere – in my native village in southern Romania; in Fayetteville, North Carolina; in a mountain town in Nepal; in Tierra del Fuego; or in New York, in Rome, or in Calcutta – all people "stand vertically," mind their daily business, and behave as if their place was the center of the world. They also smile at you and are interested in your life if you smile at them and show interest in theirs. To be sure, there are many barriers to communication. But with goodwill and a little effort, communication is possible, and with it comes a better world.

Nicholas Dima

About The Author

Nicholas Dima is a native of Romania who immigrated to the United States in 1969. A graduate of Bucharest University, Dima continued his work at Columbia University in New York, where he acquired a Ph.D. in 1975, specializing in Geography, Population, and Area Studies. After graduation, Dr. Dima engaged in teaching and research, becoming the author of three books and numerous professional articles. He has traveled widely throughout the world, and has spoken publicly on many occasions. From 1975 to 1985, Dr. Dima worked as a writer and radio reporter for Voice of America (USIA). Since 1985, he has been a visiting professor in the Foreign Area Officer Department of the United States Army John F. Kennedy Special Warfare Center and School at Fort Bragg, North Carolina. Here he was charged with teaching cross-cultural communication and he became the director of the European/Soviet Regional Studies. In 1989 Dr. Dima returned to the Voice of America.

Acknowledgements

This volume is the result of over three years of research, interacting with colleagues, and teaching cross-cultural communication to officers and enlisted personnel at the United States Army John F. Kennedy Special Warfare Center and School, Fort Bragg, North Carolina. Many persons have contributed over the years to the success of cross-cultural communication instruction and to my own enrichment. Nevertheless, for the completion of this book, I wish to acknowledge above all Lieutenant Colonel Robert H. Van Horn Jr., who authored the chapter "The American Modal Personality," and Chaplain (Major) Paul E. Barkey, who authored the chapter "The World's Religions."

I also wish to acknowledge Lieutenant Colonel Robert C. Anderson, who encouraged me to write this study, and William R. Wright who designed the front cover inspired by a drawing of Aurel David.

Chapter 1

Man, Culture, Society, And Communication

Man and Nature

Evolutionists postulate that man is nature's greatest achievement, while creationists believe that man was created by a divine force and thus is of unique intrinsic worth. Science is striving to unravel the past, and philosophers are trying to understand man's nature and to discern his future. Most of us do not have to delve into such profound questions; however, to better understand ourselves and to communicate with other men easier, some questions must be answered.

Man began to extricate himself from the bondage of nature several million years ago. Most scientists believe that man first evolved in tropical southeastern Africa and spread gradually all over the world.

Physically, man is very poorly equipped to cope with the environment and could not possibly compete with other species and survive, save for his brain capacity. Early man could not change the environment and had to change his body to cope with environmental changes, which explains the variety of human races existing in the present world. Later on, man learned how to subdue the environment and no longer had to change his body, but he never ceased to enrich himself and change his intellect. From this point of view, man is far from being a finished "product," and nobody knows in what direction he moves.

Man has continuously undergone almost imperceptible changes and, occasionally, great leaps. He produced the first tools more than 2 million years ago. He freed his hands by adopting an erect posture and he also learned how to use fire. Both discoveries were of colossal consequence in the humanization of our ancestors. It is also postulated that some 1 million years ago, early man had already moved into Europe, Asia, and Australia; thereafter, the evolution began to differ.

Modern man, or *Homo sapiens*, emerged about 100 thousand years ago, in a process which included the evolution of a greatly enlarged brain. Somewhere further north of his initial home drastic changes in the environment, particularly during the severe glacial periods, are credited with selectively enhancing human reasoning power, and compelling successive generations to adopt more sophisticated strategies in order to survive. At this time, apparently, the best location for human progress was somewhere in the Middle East. It was there, some 10,000 years ago, that man first began to abandon his precarious nomadic and precarious existence as a hunter and become a farmer. The invention of agriculture changed the face of the earth radically, changed man himself, and the world of nature around him.

As long as man has a body, made of the same materials as every other creature, he is still a part of nature, but a part with a special place, standing between nature and his creation – man-made things. Born as a completely helpless creature, he becomes man through socialization with other humans and through "culture."

Although from a physical point of view man belongs to earth, spiritually he is a unique being in the universe. At some point in his evolution, man began to believe that he also had an invisible soul which was immortal, and after death the soul would go to another realm with different laws for which he had to start to prepare in this lifetime. This may be one possible explanation for the beginning of the burials of deceased fellow men. It is the only explanation for the elaborate burial rituals of the early Egyptians. Coming on earth from nature, man lives between nature and his own artificial environment, and he dies with a belief in life after death for which he must live and behave in certain prescribed ways. A multitude of people share this belief and a few men have founded great religions with this message. Science disagrees on this account and philosophy is divided. Karl Ritter, a German geographer, even believed that a divine will created the earth as a school for man to evolve from barbarism to spiritual greatness. And we are still evolving.

Culture and Society

To survive, man has always lived in groups, and there are no groups of people without culture or culture without man. Culture could be defined as the shared experience of a group of people, which is learned through socialization and is transmitted from generation to generation in order to survive, perpetuate, and prosper. A more complete definition of culture according to *Webster's* dictionary is "the total pattern of human behavior and its products embodied in thought, speech, action, and artifacts, and dependent upon man's capacity for learning and transmitting knowledge to succeeding generations through the use of tools, language, and systems of abstract thought."[1]

Human behavior not only is a central part of culture but also one of culture's most visible elements. Patterns of behavior are typical for any given group of people and are based upon commonly held notions or ideas. Such culturally defined ideas give a particular group a sense of purpose and a common identity, which can vary from membership in a private club to membership in a large nation.

Of all human traits, perhaps the language and the power of abstract thinking are the most important and exclusively human. In order to hunt a

LAYERS OF CULTURE

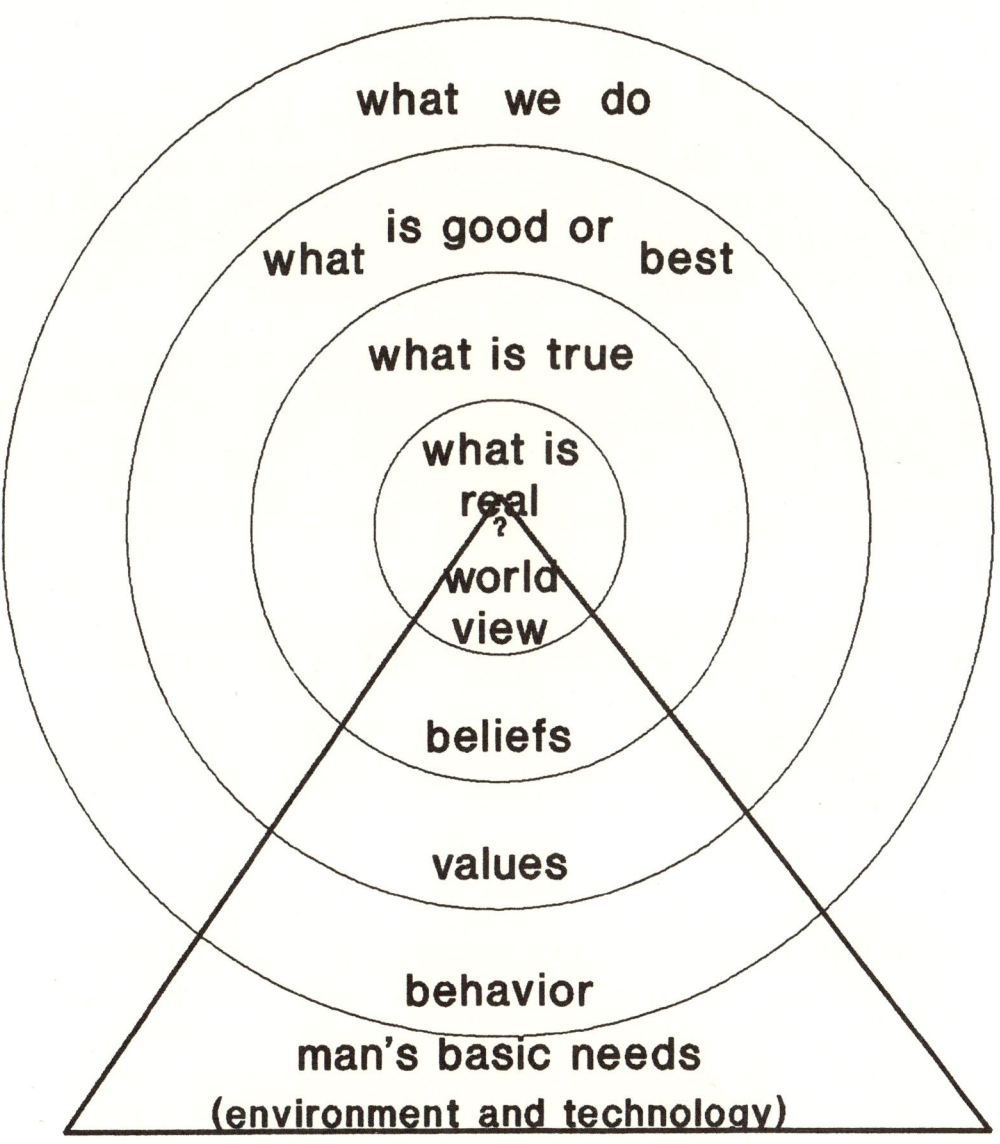

Figure 1-1

wild buffalo or a mammoth, early man had to communicate and coordinate his actions. He had to find appropriate sounds for portions of nature existing outside as well as for his inner thoughts. Then, mankind evolved into larger communities when they learned to understand each other beyond the immediate need for exchanging goods. The skill of good communication was thus important from the beginning. Later, when various communities learned the benefits of cooperation, they molded themselves into societies.

Societies implied intricate social organizations and a complex culture which began to shape everyone's personality. When such societies were stable enough, occupied a rather well-defined territory, and were controlled by a group of powerful individuals, they became "states," as known in history. Further, modern societies developed new technologies and relations of production, formed specialized institutions to cope with specific aspects of the communal life, acquired deeper knowledge, elaborated stricter norms of behavior, developed value systems and various beliefs, and eventually reached into everybody's life.

All societies function according to certain forms of social organization, which evolve from various patterns of behavior. Social organization varies on the one hand with the natural environment and level of technology, and on the other hand with the accumulated experience of the society. The unwritten expected patterns of behavior of any society are called "norms." They are embodied in folkways and mores, as well as laws, and are enforced through various social mechanisms from recognition and reward for "model" behavior to ridicule or sanction for deviations. The observance of such norms makes a smooth social interaction, while their violation creates friction and conflict. Ideally, laws that govern the functioning of modern countries should reflect the popular folkways and mores of the governed people, and in many cases they do. Otherwise, the conflict between the laws and the folkways and mores of the population could lead to destabilization and social upheaval.

One of the most stable social groupings is the modern nation and its political expression, the nation-state. The entire world is now divided among nation-states and multi-ethnic states of varying degrees of independence and interdependence. In fact, many of today's modern states are multi-ethnic and few of the existing countries today remain homogeneous, in the sense of being inhabited by one ethnic group, but we still often refer to them by the names of the major group as though they were nation-states. Nevertheless, calling all the Soviets "Russians" is not only misleading, but also would offend about 140 million Soviets who are not Russians.

There are many definitions of nationality. Unlike a nation which connotes the political nation-state, nationality refers to ethnicity, the true identity of a person within a state. Understanding what makes a specific nationality in a

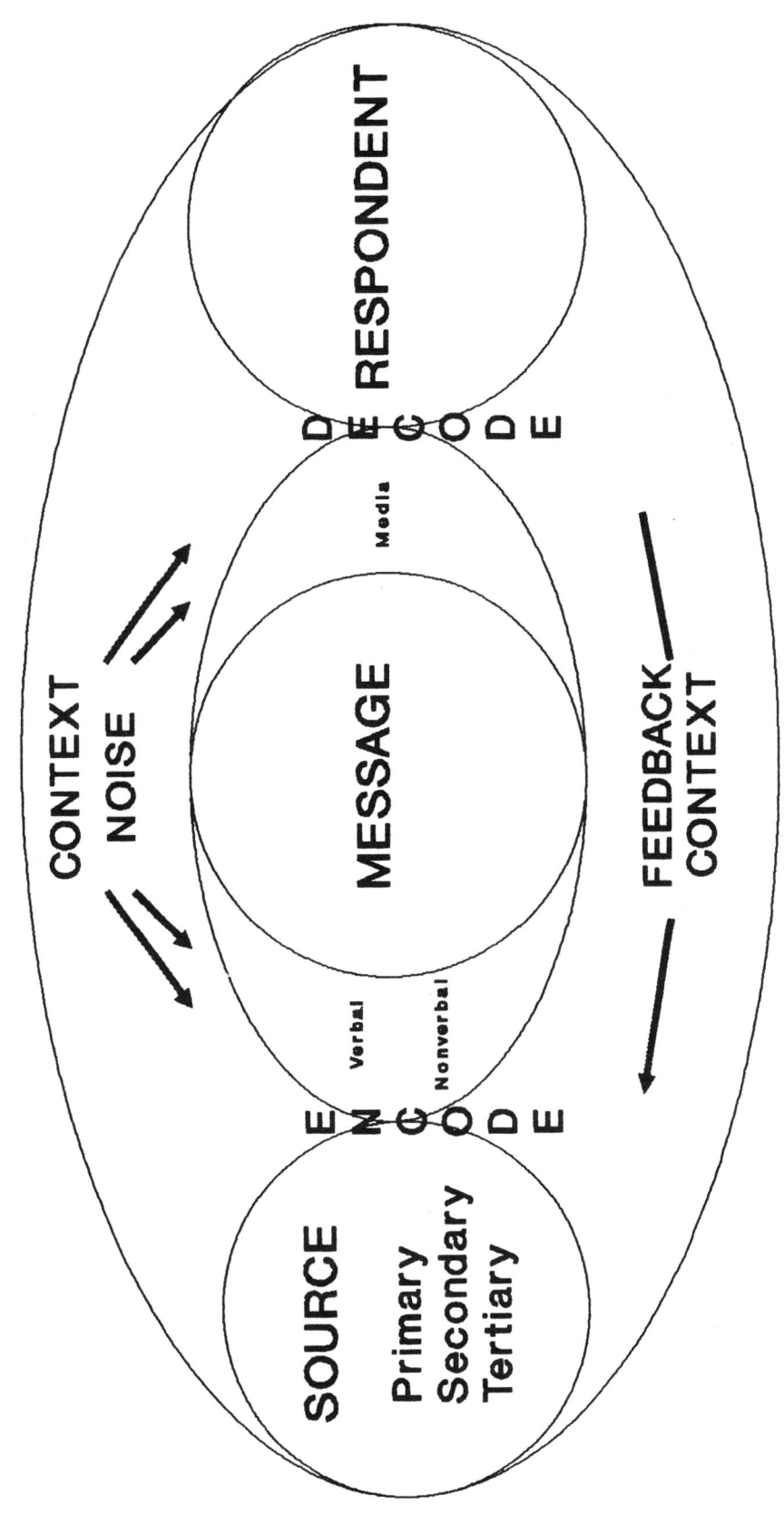

Figure 1-2

given nation-state may not be easy, but failing to know its main ingredients such as common ancestry, language, religion, traditions, etc., could lead to serious miscommunication. It is obvious that what brought the Jews back to Israel was not any common language, but their religious belief. The chief element in Switzerland appears to be their common history, while in France it is the language, the history of the people, and "la culture Française" in a more refined definition. Nevertheless, what is the common glue in Lebanon or many newly independent African countries? Failing to understand such sensitivities can gravely impede any communication.

Culture and Communication

The basic needs of all humans are similar: food, clothes, and shelter. Consequently, societies must facilitate the functioning of the group through a given culture and political institutions. All cultures, from incipient civilizations to modern nation-states, are preoccupied essentially with the same goals: They must help to produce and distribute goods and services; must maintain internal order; and must secure a place in the international arena. However, understanding a culture is never easy, particularly when cultures change continuously, and communicating is even more difficult without a good understanding.

While drinking tea in a teahouse in Jaipur, India, I began to discuss various subjects with a group of young men. For some reason, we drifted toward discussing American and Indian culture, and the talk became very interesting. I found out that the men were Brahmin, the highest Indian caste, and one of them was a priest and had his own Hindu temple. He also owned a little store with semiprecious stones, because, he pointed out, in India servants of God are not paid to perform sacred duties.

I visited his store and he showed me, among many other things, a big and beautiful amethyst. He measured the polished stone and explained the traits that a good gem should have, and we started negotiating a price. By this time, I was well versed in Indian haggling, though I still knew precious little about gems. At the same time, surrounded by a few friends and other servants of Hindu Gods, we continued to discuss culture and philosophy, though the two subjects hardly went with each other. I did not know if I truly wanted the gem, but once entering the numbers game, we kept arguing politely about the price until we ultimately agreed and I bought the amethyst. Then, I was invited into the temple where we sat down on a blanket and sipped tea. This time we discussed mostly religion and God. When inadvertently I sat with my back to the temple's altar, he pointed out politely that one should never turn his back to any God. I changed my position equally politely but asked him why he believed that God resided in his altar. He said that God resides everywhere, and that the altar was only a symbol, but as such he considered that God was

WHAT DO YOU VISUALIZE WHEN THINKING OF A TREE?

A NEW YORKER

A PUERTO RICAN

A NORTH CAROLINIAN

A CHILD

A GREENLANDER

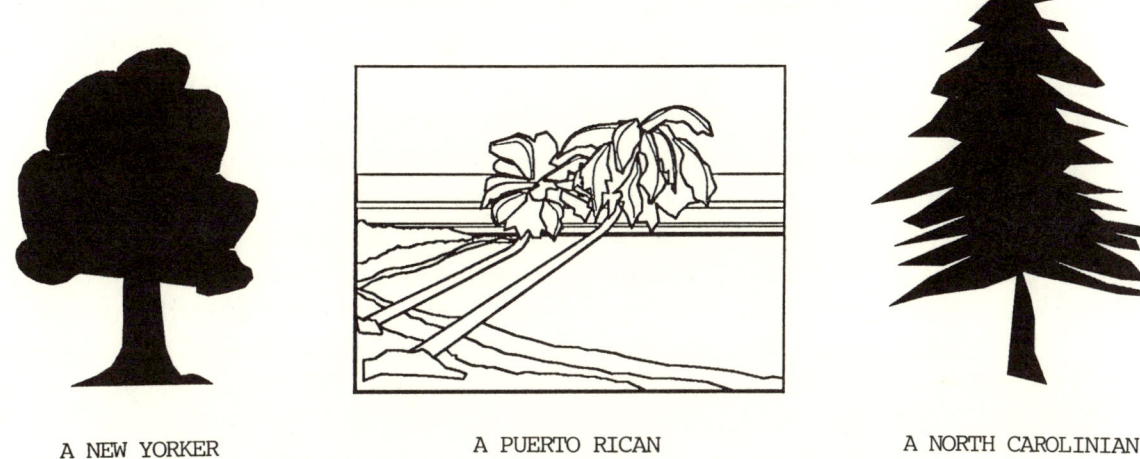

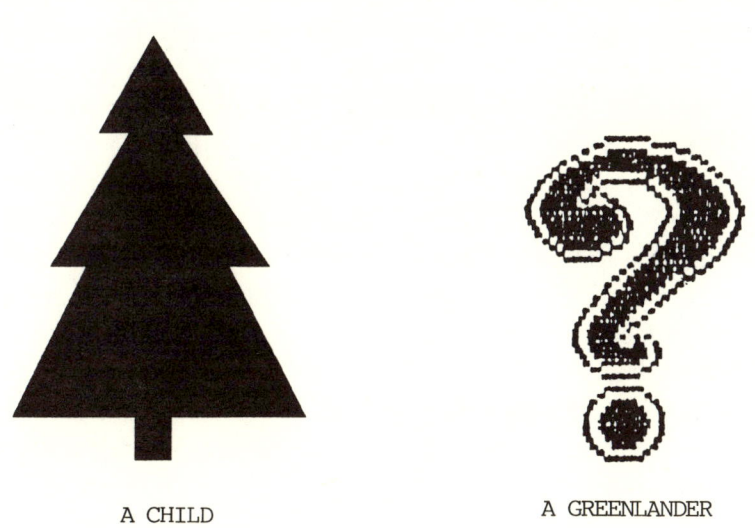

IT DEPENDS ON WHO YOU ARE AND WHERE YOU ARE FROM.

Figure 1-3

more present there than anywhere else. Then, it was his turn to ask me for a definition of God, and the discussion did not take us anywhere, except into an abstract world almost impossible to explain. What he and I had in mind were worlds apart in spite of our mutual respect and knowledge. As a Christian, I eventually had to admit that for us God is comprehensible only through Jesus Christ, and I even asked him if he would consider Jesus. To my surprise he answered serenely and immediately. "Of course I respect Jesus. He was one of many forms of God." "You should read the Bible," I continued, "and maybe you will end up believing in only one God instead of a multitude of gods." "I already read part of the Bible, and would gladly read all of it," he retorted, "but would you also read, our holy writings? Maybe I am right too."

I stopped for a while and thought of an anecdote from my native country. A man came to see the village priest and complained about both his wife and mother-in-law, whom he claimed he could not please regardless of what he did. The priest listened carefully, agreed with him, and conceded, "you are right." Not long after, the man's wife came and complained bitterly about her husband, and the priest again agreed and said, "you are right." Eventually the man's mother-in-law came and complained about being misunderstood, and the priest said again, "you are right." As an Orthodox, allowed to have a family, the priest had a daughter and she heard all those conversations and said, "But Father, you told everyone that he or she was right." "Yes," the priest admitted, "you are right, too, and this is the problem." How easy it was to negotiate a price, how painless it was to compromise, and how difficult it was to understand and reconcile our cultural differences, particularly when each of us was "right."

It was obvious that the mild-mannered and well-educated Brahmin priest and I held completely different values, beliefs, and different concepts of the world and of our places within the universe surrounding us. Late into the night, we parted as friends and I realized that it would take a tremendous effort to bridge the communication gap at such a level of abstract thought; however, by understanding there were differences was in itself a big step in opening communication.

Cultural "Pyramids"

Some researchers visualize culture as a series of concentric circles. Accordingly, the largest circle represents what men do, or man's behavior. The next circle is what is good or best for a given society, which represents its values. The next one is what is true, which gives us our beliefs.[2] The last and central circle represents what is real, or what we believe the world is like. This is a useful approach to understanding culture and ourselves. Among other things, it can explain why and where communication is easy or difficult. If

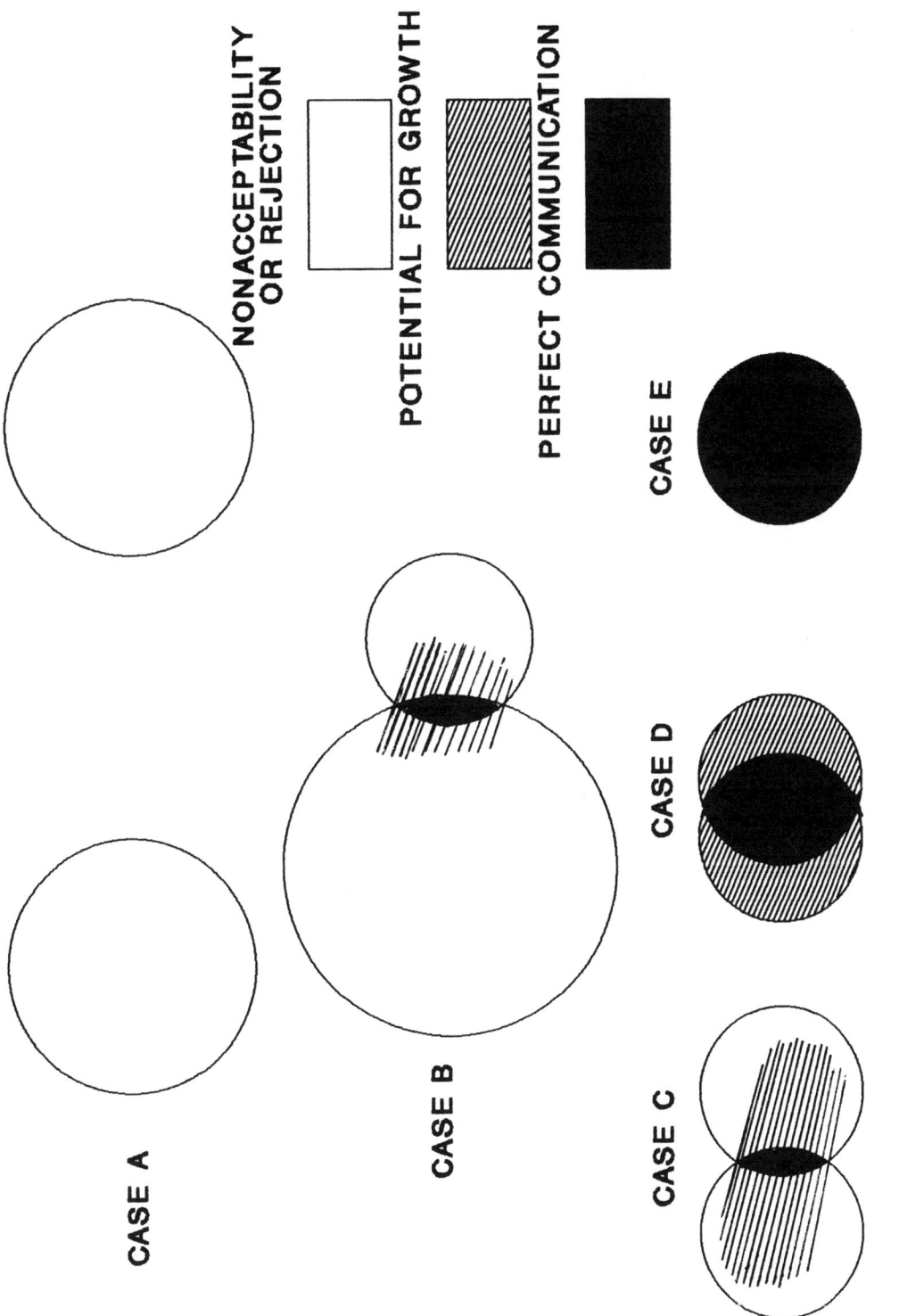

Figure 1-4

further elaborated upon and developed, it should be viewed as a three-dimensional pyramid rather than as concentric circles (see figure 1-1).

Whereas all men and cultures are primarily preoccupied with making a living – which at least means food, clothes, and shelter obtained from the earth's environment – at the base of the pyramid should be man's environment and his technology. What is done, which is our behavior to a high degree, depends then on the environment we inhabit, on the level of technology man employs to satisfy his ever-changing needs, and on our attitude toward nature. However, from the tropics to the polar regions, there is a multitude of environments, and through history societies have changed continuously. Furthermore, if one of the definitions of behavior is the peculiar reaction to certain circumstances, then from the beginning, behavior varies not only with the culture but also with the environment. Nevertheless, this is probably the sole area where we can adjust to various circumstances, or influence others, and eventually bring about a better understanding and communication.

All cultures have specific ideas and notions of what is good, beneficial, or best, which are reflected in the behavior and attitude of the people. When such notions are adopted by the majority of the people, they become the values of that particular culture. Unlike behavior, which is steadily changing, values are "preset" decisions between choices made by consensus, and they indicate what should or must be done in order to conform to the pattern of life in a given culture.[3] They are also a lot more stable and equally more difficult to break, compromise, or reconcile. In more static, traditional, less developed societies, violating basic values could result in grave consequences. Again, what is good in a given natural environment for its inhabitants may not be good in a different one. Correspondingly, the "proper" behavior and the values which people come to embrace may be equally different, and as we climb the rungs of the cultural pyramid, we ascend in different directions. Accordingly, understanding and communicating become even more difficult.

Values also reflect an underlying system of beliefs, which take us toward the pinnacle of the pyramid and which answers to what is true. Finding what is true may be one of the most difficult questions for every culture, but genuine efforts to find the truth is as important as finding it. If there is only one truth, why do our views of it vary so widely?

The sad reality is that relatively speaking, truth is neither absolute, nor permanent or universal. Nevertheless, in traditional God-centered societies, truth appears to be more stable, while in modern man-centered societies, truth appears more changing. There may be many layers of truth, and what we hold to be true is only relative, or a matter of perception, general acceptance, convenience, or sheer interest. Truth is what "we believe" and what we believe is subjective. It depends individually on the level of personal knowledge and

PERCEPTION IS IN THE EYES OF THE PERCEIVER

BUT WE CAN ALL SEE THE SAME THING

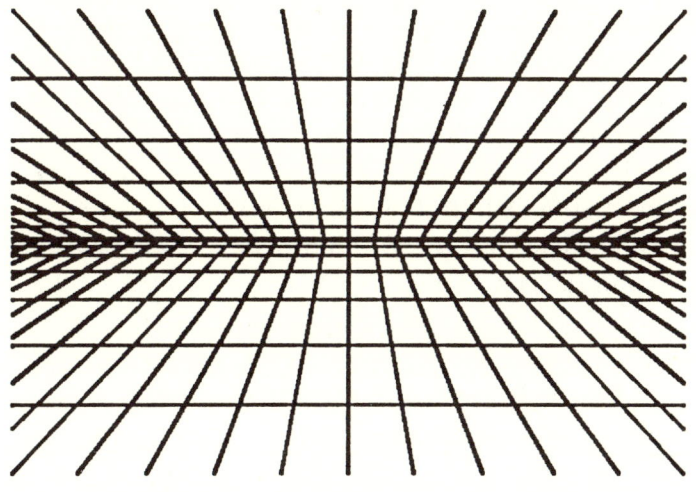

Figure 1-5

elevation, and socially on the religion of a given society, the contribution of its thinkers, and its scientific achievements. This is why changing our beliefs is painstakingly slow, and compromising them is very risky. The biggest challenge for a Christian zealot would be to convince a rabbi that Jesus was Messiah, or a devout Moslem that Mohammed was just another human with no mandate from God. Making such a blunder or gaffe can easily render a person inefficient to say the least, and communication will stop right there.

Eventually, very few of us are trying to climb to the pinnacle of the cultural pyramid in order to view the world from the top. Such a view should give one a new understanding of self, of the physical universe, and of the abstract world surrounding us. Supposedly, such a view should give one an understanding of what is real and what is unreal, except that in the depth of our minds the border between the two is blurred, and a few thinkers even reached the conclusion that "reality" is not knowable, and that we actually live in a world of perceptions. Whether this is "true" or "untrue" makes little difference, because we still have to cope with the world as various cultures and peoples perceive it.

In most cultures, the basic philosophy of life, our understanding of the world, and our place in it is governed by prevailing religions, philosophy, and science. All cultures explain, in one way or another, man's place in cosmos, and the most advanced cultures have complex and intriguing views of man's mission in the universe. In Christian societies, for example, it is almost impossible to break away completely from traditional Judeo-Christian views whether or not we adhere to Christian beliefs. We are influenced by the basic Christian values.

Our worldview is not necessarily reality itself, but rather what we accept as reality. This is true with all cultures, because each culture is as self-centered as each nation is ethnocentric. Science has made quantum leaps in more recent times to give us a better understanding of the physical world and of ourselves, but various cultures still stick to their views. While physicists are penetrating the most intimate particles of matter and astronomers are probing the "edge" of the universe, philosophers are trying hard to develop a Theory of Everything in order to unravel the ultimate truth once and for all. But is there an ultimate truth? For Hegel, for example, history moves through conflict and contradiction of ideas, and the truth unfolds gradually. There are very few people who climb the cultural pyramid to the top and add a few more "bricks" to its pinnacle. Overwhelmingly, most of us adhere to the beliefs already set up for us and to the values prevailing in our given cultures. Our behavior, however, is goal oriented in our daily activities, and as such it is greatly influenced by both our environment and technology, as well as by our beliefs and values. Moreover, since cultures are integrated systems, our environment

PERCEPTIONS! PERCEPTIONS!

IS THIS THE SAME WORLD?

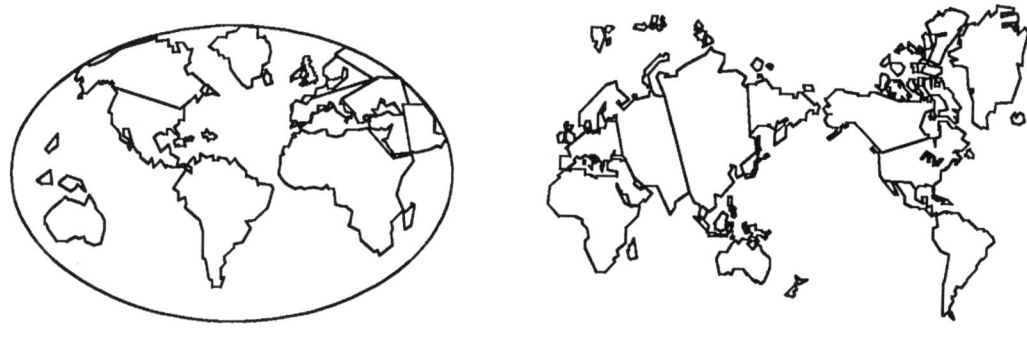

WHICH COUNTRY IS BIGGER?

GREAT BRITAIN, ACCORDING TO A JAMAICAN WHOM I MET IN KINGSTON.

Figure 1-6

and technology guide our behavior, which in turn shape our values, which further influence our beliefs. In exchange, our world view gives us our beliefs, which set up limits for our values, which in turn guide our daily behavior and our attitude toward the environment. Multitudes of people are contributing to our cultures. Aware or unaware, we are all trying to climb up the pyramid, and a few of us are able to reach the top and raise it farther. Then, the few that reach the top can bring about new beliefs and values on all of us. Such is the case with noted scientists, recognized philosophers, and, above all, founders of great religions.

Eastern religions, such as Hinduism, Buddhism, and Confucianism, have been developed by man's efforts to understand the universe and the place of man in it. They elaborated a system of beliefs and values, as well as norms of conduct and behavior meant to contribute to social harmony and personal fulfillment. From this point of view, they represent some of the most complex and intriguing philosophies of life man has ever developed.

Western religions (Judaism, Christianity, and Islam), however, are taken as revelations from God to reclaim and redeem us. They do not represent man's efforts of understanding, but rather gifts from God. Either way, nevertheless, they occupy extremely important places in man's everyday life and can act as barriers or bridges to understanding and communicating.

Culture appears as many pyramids, with the earth as their common base for the entire mankind, and a multitude of invisible pinnacles reaching to the heavens, each one representing a different culture. While it is easy to count numbers and compromise cross-culturally in the visible world of goods and services around us, with every rung of the pyramid we climb up it is more difficult to understand each other, to communicate, and to agree. Metaphorically speaking, when one reaches the top, he stands by himself, and the reality at that level – out of reach for the others – is what he "believes" reality is. We can only accept it or reject it according to our cultures and our personalities.

Communication[4]

Communication is a complex phenomenon and a dynamic process. It implies the transmission of ideas, thoughts, and feelings from one person to another. It involves a transmitter or a source, a message which is transmitted verbally or nonverbally, and a receiver or respondent (see figure 1-2). Although values and beliefs are also transmitted along with knowledge (ideas and thoughts), the immediate intent of any communication is to influence behavior. Communication is also highly symbolic. The simplest word a communicator utters, for example, could be fully understood only by those who have attached to it the same meaning as he has. The sound or written symbol "tree" might be perceived as an oak tree in Upstate New York, a palm tree in

Florida, a pine tree in North Carolina, and a "blank" in Greenland (see figure 1-3). Consequently, since a good part of the message travels through linguistic symbols (abstract codifications of reality), part of the message is always lost in the process of encoding and decoding. Thus, communication is never perfect or 100 percent successful.

Whereas communication elicits a response, it always involves at least two persons. If the two persons belong to the same culture and share the same language, the process is greatly facilitated by similar backgrounds, assumptions, and perceptions. In an ideal situation, when two persons have known each other for a long time and share most of everything, the perfect means of communication is "silence" (see figure 1-4, Case E). The need for words and for the transmission of ideas arises only when there is a difference. Whenever there is a difference, however, an effort must be made to bridge it; consequently, communication implies a certain degree of pain most of the time. If a particular group of students, for example, would know everything a professor can offer, there would be no need for communication. But usually, there is a difference, and this is just why both professors and students get together. In order to bridge the gap, the professor must make an effort to properly transmit his knowledge to the minds of the students, and the students must make an effort to understand it.

When communication takes place between two persons speaking two different languages, the process is further complicated by the culture behind the language, even though the two communicators might speak a common language. Cross-cultural communication implies, thus, an exchange of ideas between persons belonging to two different cultures, even though they use the same language. The main gap is not necessarily in the language, which eventually can be learned, but in the two cultures, produced by different environments, in which people perceive reality differently and cling to different values and beliefs. International communication is a particular case of cross-cultural communication. Most of the time, it means political communication at a governmental level or on behalf of a government.

Individual behavior is largely based on the perception of the external world, which in turn is both determined by individual biology and learned from one's cultural environment. Perception is also described as the variance between what a person believes is "real" and what is "actually real." Since no two persons are alike – they do not have exactly the same background and knowledge, and do not perceive the outside reality the same way – we are bound to misunderstand (see figures 1-5 and 1-6). Hypothetically, the more similar our cultural background and the way we perceive the outside world, the easier our communication. Contrariwise, the more different our cultural background and perceptions of reality, the more difficult it is to communicate.

Suppose now that we have two men who come from completely different places and cultures. Hypothetically, it is the year 1900 and there is no radio and television. A third party brings together a man from an isolated valley in Papua New Guinea (which in reality was discovered by the outside world only in the 1930's) and another one from northeastern Siberia, who had never left his village and hunting area. What would those two persons share and what would they communicate to each other? At best, they would be able to communicate the biological feelings that bind together the entire mankind: hunger, thirst, pain, or satisfaction (see figure 1-4, Case A). Thus, COMMUNICATION IS ONLY POSSIBLE WHEN THERE IS SOMETHING IN COMMON AND THE NEED AND DESIRE TO COMMUNICATE.

Suppose again that we are now in present-day New York. A physicist who is trying hard to elaborate upon Einstein's theory of relativity in order to apply it to the whole physical world comes across a humble, semiliterate laborer who barely makes a living. What could they communicate? In this case, the two have many things in common, but communication would mainly be in one direction and implies WILLINGNESS on the part of the physicist, OPENNESS on the part of the unfortunate man, and a great deal of PATIENCE for both (see figure 1-4, Case B).

Between such extremes, most men overlap their background and knowledge to varying degrees (see figure 1-4, Cases C and D). Wherever they overlap there is a zone of COMMUNICATION and mutual understanding which could be slowly and gradually expanded into the ACCEPTANCE zone. However, when our perceptions and beliefs are very different and our background and knowledge far away from each other, we come across a zone of REJECTION, where communication is impossible. If such varied backgrounds and perceptions of reality are confounded by different ideas of "normal versus deviant," "good versus bad," "beautiful versus ugly," and other values – valid only to specific cultures – our attempt at communication can end up in complete failure. To further understand why cultures are so different, one should start from the bottom of the pyramid and try to discern the role played by history and geography in their evolution, and to see if there is any hope for better communication in the future.

ENDNOTES

1. *Webster's Third International Dictionary* (Springfield, MA: G&C Merriam Co. Publishers, 1969), p. 552.
2. Lloyd E. Kwast, "Understanding Culture," in *Perspective on the World Christian Movement*, Ralph D. Winter, ed. (Pasadena, CA: William Carey Publishing, 1981), p. 363.
3. *Ibid*, p. 362.
4. For this section see among others: David J. Hesselgrave, *Communicating Christ Cross-Culturally*

(Grand Rapids, MI: Zondervan Publishing House 1978), chapter 4; Larry A. Samovar and Richard E. Porter, *Intercultural Communication: A Reader* (Belmont, CA: Wadsworth Publishing Co. Inc., 1976); John C. Condon and Fahti S. Yousef, *An Introduction to Intercultural Communication* (Indianapolis, IN: Bobbs-Merrill Educational Publishing, 1977); and Carley H.N. Dodd, *Perspective on Cross-Cultural Communication* (Dubuque, IA: Kendal/Hunt Publishing Co., 1977).

Chapter 2
Technological Progress, Cultural Change, and Communication

Introduction

When one travels long distances, he not only visits various geographical places, but, in a way, he also travels in history. At the same time, living long enough, one does not have to travel at all to notice the unmistakable changes that have occurred in his environment and culture within his own life. CHANGE is the permanent state of mankind. For an eastern European like myself, when I immigrated to the United States I felt like I was traveling forward in time and experiencing the future. It was a great challenge, and I had to make a big effort to leap forward and "catch up" with time. Years later, I traveled to Latin America and spent a few days in a village in Mexico. I felt like I was traveling back in time, reliving my own childhood in rural Romania. It is obvious that what makes man's cultures so diverse is not man's biology as much as geography and history – adaptation to and modification of various environments in a fourth dimension called "time." Where do we come from, and where are we heading? Is there a predestined direction and a purpose in history? Are we all advancing in the same direction? What can we do to better understand each other and to cooperate as a family of humans? These questions might be highly academic, but they do have practical implications and consequences which affect virtually everybody. Understanding them can also help us communicate better with each other across cultural barriers.

Preagricultural Man and Society

From various archeological and historical sources, as well as various studies of former or still existing preagricultural man, scientists have arrived at a good understanding of primitive societies. To be sure, such societies were neither savage nor primitive, and showed an unexpected level of cultural complexity given their limited knowledge and technology. However, if we generally agree that the agricultural revolution was man's first technological leap, which radically changed the world, in order to better understand ourselves, we must start with the distant past.

Early man was subordinate to his environment. His tools and technology were primitive. With his limited knowledge and technology he could not subdue the world of nature around him, and was obliged to submit to its blind forces. As a nomad, scavenger, gatherer and hunter, always on the move in search of the next meal, his freedom was restricted by the harshness of the environment. To satisfy his simple needs, early man lived in small groups of no more than 50 to 100 individuals. In those days, women of the group were dependent to a large degree on the men of the group and gave birth to many children of whom only very few survived to perpetuate the group. Within such small groups the cohesion had to be strong. In spite of the evolutionary abused rule of the survival of the fittest, everyone depended on each other for survival.

Early human behavior must have been rather close to that of the animal kingdom. Family in the modern American sense did not exist, and the children belonged to their mothers and the entire group. Social organization was very simple, and the stronger and more intelligent man was probably the leader of the group. People were ignorant, fatalistic, and fearful of natural catastrophes that they could not understand or explain. Life was precarious, insecure, and a permanent struggle (see figures 2-1 and 2-2).

The time concept for primitive man was divided between day and night, and cold, warm, or rainy seasons, as well as childhood, maturity, and old age. Life expectancy was extremely short, and death was so common that it did not mean much to anybody. There was no concept of personal property to be valued, and survival must have been the highest value of this age. Although the belief system began to take shape rather early in the minds of our ancestors, in the absence of a well-defined "world view," they must have been rather nebulous. Yet, it was this primitive man who – after thousands upon thousands of years of slow accumulation of knowledge – learned to grow food and herd animals. Man eventually learned that people did not have to move continuously for food, but could bring the food "home" and settle on their "farms."

In the beginning, primitive societies must have been rather similar from a cultural point of view, because they were the result of the same environment that imposed upon them a very limited number of options. The language of such people was unquestionably simple with a small number of words, and inasmuch as cooperation was possible, communication was easy. However, with a brain capacity similar to ours, by the time early man discovered agriculture, he was already a complex creature and his culture diversified.

Agricultural Age

The domestication of plants and animals began some 10 thousand years ago, most likely in the Middle East. What exactly prompted this paramount invention is not known precisely, although it is established that when it occurred, tools were more sophisticated and technology more advanced. Once invented, agriculture spread through diffusion and migration and reached out to the adjacent regions and eventually to most of the world. The consequences for both man and environment were extraordinary. First, it put a price on cultivable land and with it the idea of private property. Then, it made possible permanent settlements as small villages in the middle of the land or along various fertile valleys. The idea of family and marriage came into being, though the traditional family was much larger than modern families and might have included several blood relatives working and living together. In time, settled communities were capable of producing enough food to free others from daily chores, allowing them to concentrate on other pursuits.

Agricultural communities grew considerably to reach thousands of people who learned to live together, to cooperate, and to communicate. Agricultural man could not control the environment yet, but was well embarked on a course of subduing it through deforestation, planted fields, irrigation systems, and huge constructions. With plenty of land still available, families were large and children were considered desirable assets. Women were in a subordinated position, but they were the heart of the household and would usually give birth to as many children as nature itself decided. Nevertheless, with the diseases, epidemics, and recurring natural disasters, mortality was high, average life expectancy was still short, and most children would die in infancy.

Rural societies were a lot more complex than the previous groups. They developed intricate social institutions which gradually came to govern the entire society. Behavior was profoundly affected by the adoption of agriculture. With the new crop calendar, a new time concept came into being, and permanent and new work habits were formed. Most people were still illiterate, but the accumulation of knowledge forced a need for systematization and writing. While cities developed and small city-states grew to cover huge areas, administration and the military art were greatly enhanced.

In the realm of values and beliefs, these societies produced complex, complete, and lasting systems. The new values, for example, were shaped by both the behavior imposed by the invention of agriculture and by the great thinkers who enriched the cultural pyramid and imposed their ideas from above. Interestingly, some of the greatest philosophers of mankind such as Plato, Aristotle, Socrates in the West, and Confucius in the East, lived during this age of mankind. At the same time, all the major religions of the modern world were established during the agricultural age. No important religion was established thereafter. Hinduism – which is equally religion and philosophy – as well as Judaism are thousands of years old. Buddhism is an offspring of Hinduism and appeared some 500 years before Jesus, while Islam was founded about A.D. 600. Judaism, Hinduism, Buddhism, Christianity, and Islam gave mankind complete explanations of the universe and the role and mission of man, as well as systems of beliefs, values, and norms of conduct and behavior, which are still prevalent in most of the world today.

Whereas it may be hypothesized that preagricultural societies were little differentiated, the conquest of the earth through agriculture has led to a great diversity of cultures – many of them self-contained, developed in isolation, and occasionally antagonistic to each other in their beliefs and value systems.

Communication between such a diversity of cultures was hardly possible. Whenever two such different cultures would collide, the stronger imposed his will and values upon the weaker. The modern concepts of "territorial integrity" or worldwide "human rights" were unknown. Behind the behavior of the intruders were not necessarily hidden or evil designs, but irreconcilable values. When the first colonists came to the New World, for example, the collision with the local Indians was inevitable. As agriculturists, the colonists prized and claimed land as private property, whereas the Indians did not have such a concept. As another example, Christian missionaries treated with contempt any other religion, without studying or considering its merits, and Islam was imposed mercilessly by Mohammed's disciples.

Industrial Revolution

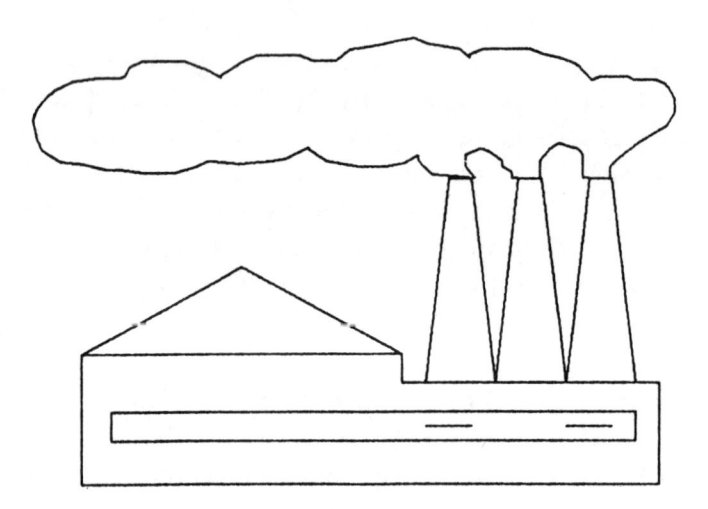

Whereas the agricultural revolution took thousands of years until it was adopted throughout the whole world, the Industrial Revolution, which began less than 300 years ago, struck the world like thunder. It began in England, spread to Western Europe, then to "overseas Europe," and eventually caught up with the rest of the world. Instead of adapting to new environments, the new revolution "brought" the environment to man in the form of minerals, energy, and raw materials. It made possible large-scale industrial activities and huge urban agglomerations. It gave Europe an impetus and a lead over the

MAJOR CHANGES IN MAN'S TECHNOLOGY AND CULTURE

WHERE FROM? ───▷ WHERE TO?

| 100,000 YEARS | 8000 B.C. | A.D. 1700 | POST WWII |
| MODERN MAN | MIDDLE EAST | ENGLAND | USA |

PRIMITIVE AGE	AGRICULTURAL AGE	INDUSTRIAL AGE	INFORMATION AGE
SIMPLE TECHNOLOGY	IMPROVED TECHNOLOGY	COMPLEX TECHNOLOGIES	HIGH TECHNOLOGY
FOOD GATHERING AND HUNTING	FOOD PRODUCING	MANUFACTURING	SERVICING
NOMADISM AND MIGRATIONS	PERMANENT SETTLEMENTS	LARGE URBAN CONCENTRATIONS	SUBURBAN GROWTH
NO PRIVATE PROPERTY	PRIVATE PROPERTY	PRIVATE/INDUSTRIAL PROPERTY	PRIVATE/PUBLIC/CORP. PROPERTY
ADAPTATION TO ENVIRONMENT	CHANGE OF ENVIRONMENT	CONTROL OF ENVIRONMENT	ENVIRONMENTAL FREEDOM
STRONG GROUP AFFINITIES	STRONG FAMILY TIES	NUCLEAR FAMILIES	LOOSE FAMILY TIES
GROUP MENTALITY	FAMILY MENTALITY	INDIVIDUALISM	SELFISHNESS
DEPENDENT WOMEN	SUBORDINATED WOMEN	COOPERATIVE WOMEN	INDEPENDENT WOMEN
FEAR AND FATALISM	COMPLEX RELIGIONS	RATIONALISM, SECULARIZATION	SCIENCE AND LOGIC
SURVIVAL OF THE FITTEST	SURVIVAL OF THE GROUP	SURVIVAL OF THE NATION	SURVIVAL OF THE WORLD
UNSTABLE AND INSECURE LIFE	STABLE SOCIETIES	DESTABILIZED AND MOBILE	HIGH MOBILITY
ILLITERATE AND IGNORANT	ILLITERATE, KNOWLEDGEABLE	FORMAL EDUCATION	SPECIALIZED EDUCATION
NO TIME CONCEPT	AGRICULTURAL CALENDARS	MODERN TIME (THE CLOCK)	PRECISE (ELECTRONIC) TIME
RESTRICTED FREEDOM	ECOLOGICAL LIMITATIONS	ENVIRONMENTAL FREEDOM	EARTH-FREE

| AGRICULTURAL | INDUSTRIAL REVOLUTION | INFORMATION |
| REVOLUTION | (US: 1860-1918) | REVOLUTION |

Figure 2-1

Compiled by Dr. Nicholas Dima
USAJFKSWCS, January 1987

CULTURAL TREND OF MANKIND: CAUSES AND CONSEQUENCES

(WESTERN EXPERIENCE)

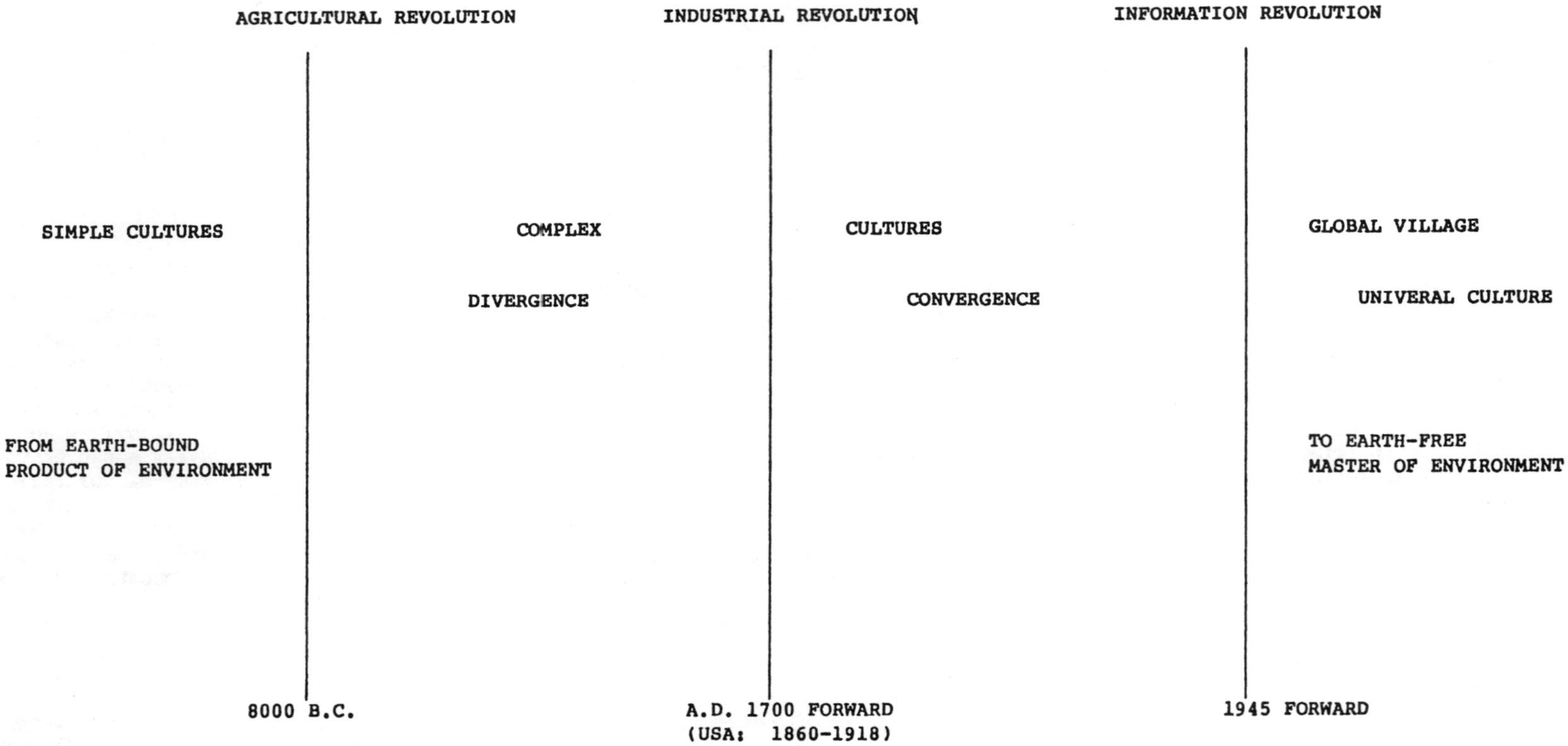

AGRICULTURAL REVOLUTION	INDUSTRIAL REVOLUTION	INFORMATION REVOLUTION
COMPLEX	CULTURES	GLOBAL VILLAGE
DIVERGENCE	CONVERGENCE	UNIVERAL CULTURE
		TO EARTH-FREE
		MASTER OF ENVIRONMENT
8000 B.C.	A.D. 1700 FORWARD (USA: 1860-1918)	1945 FORWARD

SIMPLE CULTURES

FROM EARTH-BOUND
PRODUCT OF ENVIRONMENT

Figure 2-2

Compiled by Dr. Nicholas Dima
USA|FKSWCS, January 1987

entire world, which it kept until the end of the Second World War. Most important, however, the new revolution caused painful transformations, collisions of values, and cultural adjustments with which most of the world is still wrestling.

The Industrial Revolution led eventually to what has been called "modernization," which involves steady economic development on the one hand, and permanent population adjustment on the other. As an adjustment to new economic needs and opportunities, rural population is redistributed to cities and industrial sites. While adjusting to new functions of modern society, people undergo profound psychological changes with new stresses on individualism and personal achievements. Chief economic activities are also moved from family or kinship to specialized organizations and from local settings to national institutions.

The proliferation of knowledge and the new economic activities made formal schooling a must, which, in turn, opened up the modern societies to vertical mobility. The modern and complex technology helped man subdue the environment to a degree unknown in the past, and sometimes with grave consequences. "Machinism" also imposed a new behavior, while the accumulated knowledge and political philosophy gave mankind a better understanding of itself and of the universe. The new revolution also introduced more equalitarian attitudes into Western societies, rationalism instead of fatalism, and secular institutions instead of religion. While the new man was freed to a high degree from the vagaries of the environment, his pace of life was greatly accelerated by the new technology. With most industrial activities revolving around the clock, a new time concept was needed and adopted, forcing upon societies a punctuality never known before. Additionally, the new families became smaller and even nuclear, and the woman has become a partner rather than a subordinated person, well on her way to emancipation.

The ever-changing technology has continuously forced adjustments of behavior at the bottom of the cultural pyramid. At the same time, science began to compete with God for the minds of the people, often offering contradictory systems of values and beliefs. Man was squeezed and confused between the base and the pinnacle of his changing cultural pyramid, oftentimes resulting in personal frustration or social upheaval.

With ideas about the brotherhood of all men finding their way into the minds of many thinkers, the old tribal societies and nation states tended to be replaced by multi-ethnic political states. The Roman Empire was an early example of this. These political states acquired their own reasons for being and their survival became the main preoccupation of their leaderships. In the end, after two devastating world wars, mankind found itself thrown into another age.

In spite of all its negative aspects, the Industrial Revolution brought about material progress, higher standards of living, new aspirations of freedom and prosperity, and a great increase of communication. If invention of agriculture and its horizontal expansion brought cultural diversity, industrialization brought along a convergence of cultures with more tolerance toward diversity and more mutual understanding. Certain institutions, such as compulsory schooling, university education, similar governmental activities, and trade and international organizations, made communication easier, at least among opinion leaders worldwide. Vis-a-vis the same machines, trains, radios, appliances, etc., all men must resort to somewhat similar forms of behavior. If education, for example, helps a member of a poor family join the middle class, education becomes a universal value. At the other end of the cultural spectrum, science and a much better scientific understanding of the universe also bring educated people closer. Religion still keeps us apart, but unlike in the agricultural past, religion is becoming a private rather than a national pursuit for many people in the modern world. Nevertheless, the globalization and internationalization of the world brought about by the Industrial Revolution facilitated new avenues for communication between people of various cultures. Whereas the agricultural age kept people isolated and focused on the land, the industrial age encouraged mankind to think in global terms. At the same time, the world has moved from a God-centered traditionalist view toward a man-centered one (see figure 2-3).

The Information Revolution

Every revolution had been the result of the efforts of the people living in the previous stage. No culture could foresee the consequences of its own efforts, except probably for a handful of visionaries who might have been capable of imagining vaguely the next stage. However, once a new stage was implanted, it revolutionized and changed drastically everything behind. Consequently, sometime during the first part of this century, a new revolution began, first in the minds of some brilliant people. It is difficult to pin-point exactly when it started, but somewhere between the first atomic explosion of 1945 and the incredible landing of an American astronaut on the moon in 1969, mankind entered upon a new historical course. Though, it still does not have a certified name, most people call it the "information revolution." It implies a new technology called High Tech, and an incredible spread of knowledge and information around the whole world.

The new technology coming of age is so complex and improves so rapidly, that it is said that if an average person understands it, it is already obsolete. On the one hand, computers, semiconductors, superconductors, biochips, and a whole array of new technologies make communication easy and instant

A MAN-CENTERED WORLD IS REPLACING

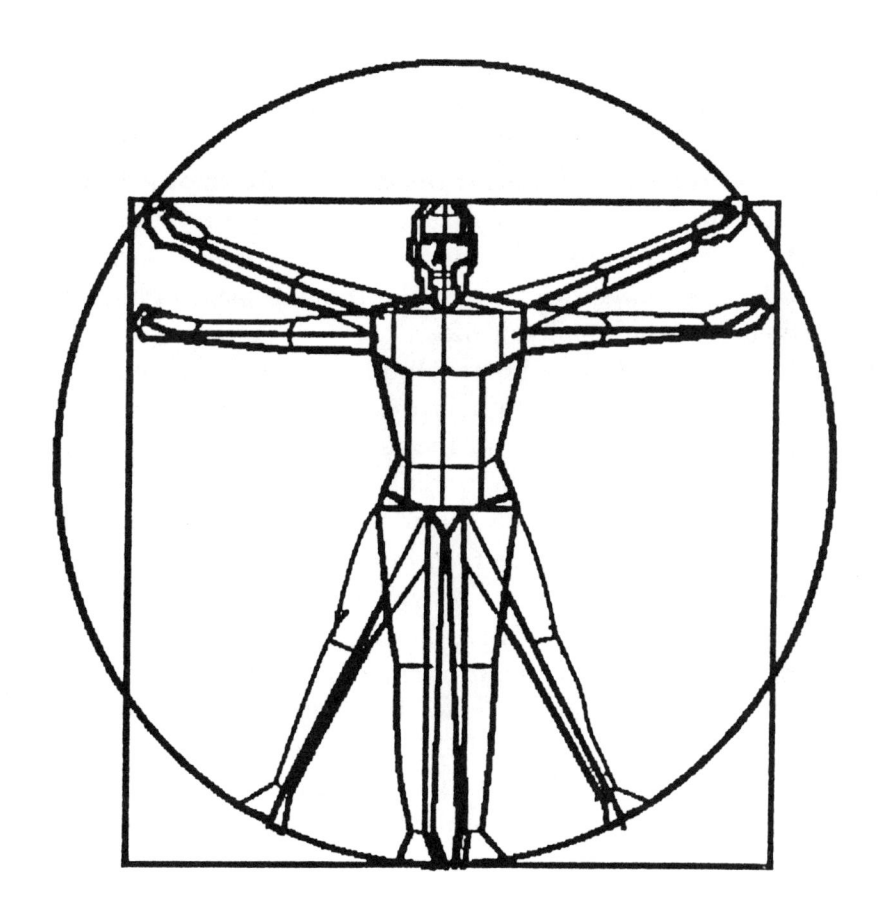

THE TRADITIONALIST GOD-CENTERED VIEW

Figure 2-3

globally. On the other hand, science is unraveling the most intimate structure of the matter and is probing the beginning and the end of the known universe. Furthermore, new frontier sciences are ready for the colonization of space, and biogenetics are looking for new forms of life to be created, producing what appears to be an earth-free man.

The new age has created great adjustment problems for the whole world. The implications and consequences are impossible to foresee, but they will change the world profoundly with both good and bad consequences. Traditional smoke-stack industries of high scale are being replaced with modern computerized ones, smaller and more efficient. Industry in general is being replaced by services. Successful individuals are more knowledgeable, more specialized, and can work most anyplace rather than performing in a factory. Consequently, the big cities of the Western World might be ultimately replaced by suburban developments with new emphasis being placed on the quality of the environment and the quality of life.

On the negative side, the new revolution, which is sweeping the carpet from under our feet, has come with new pressures and demands. Women have acquired legal parity with men and the family is no longer a natural and economically necessary unit. The old traditional values are being discarded, the new morality is loose, and the new ethics and values are yet to consolidate. Moreover, not every country or every citizen is benefiting from the new age, and the frustration is giving way to violence and international tension. Incapable of competing with the West, the Communist countries attempted to force utopian solutions which made them more antagonistic to their own people and to the free democratic world. At the same time, developing countries, threatened with losing their traditions and identities, resort to counterrevolutions trying to revive the old values. This is the case with religious fundamentalism in such countries as Iran, where, in disregard of global trends, the clergy is opposing modernization.

Scientists agree, however, that there is no way to cope with future shock unless we change our old ways. The future world – that is, the world of the next century – will become more international and global in perspective as we struggle to survive. Transnational corporations are gaining a dominant role in business, and national interests are becoming increasingly compromised by international interests. The pattern of the agricultural sector, for example, will probably no longer resemble the farms of today. Agriculture will probably constitute a specialized form of business activity conducted from a remote computer that will talk to other computers, select the best crops and varieties of seed for a given track of land, and then arrange with various enterprises for the plowing, sowing, fertilizing, and harvesting of the crops. Many of the specialists involved would no longer have to understand the whole picture, and storing, transporting, marketing, or processing would be equally done by specialized firms working from equally distant places. All this might be sad in a way, but change is the price mankind is continuously paying for having eaten the apple from the Garden of Eden. I personally believe that the traditional American family farm will have a hard time adjusting to future shock.

We are in the midst of a revolution and, as always under such times, there is anguish associated with the transition. And there are winners and there are losers, but there is also a new man in the making. In spite of the fact that inside each one of us there is a the primeval urge for the peacefulness of village life, there is also the attraction of civilized urbanity. We have to become more knowledgeable and more ready to discover other peoples' view-points. There is a need for more understanding and more communication, in order to fit into tomorrow's world, and hopefully make it a better place.

This model of global evolution is still applicable only to the Western experience, but I believe that it shows the destiny of the entire mankind. The entire world is inevitably moving toward modern technology. Japan and a few other Pacific-rim countries are already engaged on the same path. Will the Third World countries follow the same route? Do they have any other choice or a separate destiny? Visitors of the distant Papua New Guinea speak of naked men walking along ancient trails listening to transistors and jumping to the rhythm of rock-and-roll music. How many people resisted the temptation of owning a TV set, or are not considering buying a VCR if they do not already have two of them by now? How many "primitive" people in Amazonia would not want to have a color TV and a dish antenna to watch a music show from Nashville, Tennessee? Once a discovery was made or an invention was adopted, it left no choice for the rest of the world except to follow suit.

This model does not answer to such crucial questions as where we come from or where we are heading. Astronomer Carl Sagan hypothesized that civilization might end up in self-destruction. In order to avoid such a catastrophic end, communication is highly necessary and possible, but what should be the common ground?

Common Ground for Communication

The beauty and the puzzle of this world is that at the close of the 20th century, we will still have societies living at a preagricultural level, alongside agricultural, industrial, and post-industrial societies. Horizontal communication between societies sharing a close technology and compatible values and beliefs is easier, except that if they compete for the same thing they could collide with each other with grave consequences. Vertical communication between societies at different technological levels had been one of subordination in the past, and one full of quarreling and arguing at present. A drastic conflict between such societies, however, is less catastrophic than the previous case, because the weak ones have no choice but to submit to the strong ones. Communication over a large gap, such as between post-industrial societies and agricultural ones, is more difficult and usually takes place between persons trained to have something in common.

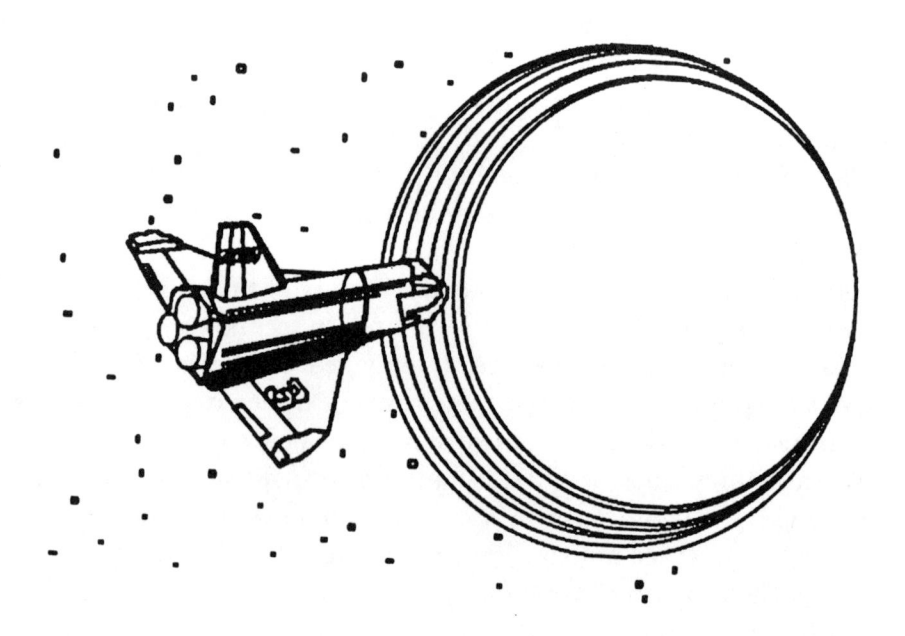

If mankind is to survive and prosper, there is no substitute for *mutual respect, tolerance of diversity, goodwill, patience,* and *openness*. We are already engaged on a road of global cultural understanding, paved by increasing education, science, accumulation of knowledge, and more humanitarian attitudes. If all humans have the same basic needs and share similar personality traits, as well as a common destiny, some common ground for understanding should be found and should be expanded. The pursuit of happiness is universal, although its makeup may differ from culture to culture. It implies, nevertheless, a decent material standard of living, freedom, opportunities, and choices. Spiritual meaning, or the search for it, is hardly tangible and more personal. However, as long as individuals communicate at the lower levels of the cultural pyramid and manage to secure freedom and a decent standard of living, they can be left to bring their unique contribution to the upper layers of the pyramid, climb to its pinnacle, erect it further, and find their own spiritual fulfillment. Then, they can share it with the rest of us. And maybe one day mankind will eventually realize that we are all alike, and only our ways are different. Then, cross-cultural communication will no longer be a problem.

REFERENCES

This chapter is, in a way, an outgrowth of the first chapter (Purpose, Approach, and Hypotheses) of the author's own doctoral dissertation on population and social change. In addition, a multitude of current sources have been used for the study of the present social change. Here are a few references for the transformation of rural societies into industrial societies and their implications:

Donald J. Bogue
Principles of Demography (New York: John Wiley and Sons, 1969).
Donald Cowgill
"Transition Theory as General Population Theory," *Social Forces*, 41 (October 1962).
Peter F. Drucker
"The Changing World Economy," *Foreign Affairs* (Spring 1986).
Calvin Goldscheider
Population, Modernization, and Social Structure (Boston: Little, Brown and Company, 1971).
Stanley A. Hetzler
Technological Growth and Social Changes (London: Routledge and Kegan Paul, 1969).
Everett S. Lee
"A Theory of Migration," *Demography*, III, No. 1 (1966).
E. A. Wrigley
Population and History (London: Weidenfeld and Nicolson, World University Library, 1969).

Chapter 3
Personality Formation And Communication

Introduction

Human personality is the result of interaction between several factors, of which the most important are:

- Inherited traits.

- Cultural environment.

- Unique experience in life.

Each newborn begins with a certain potential that is genetically inherited. Yet, he becomes "human" only through socialization with other humans or through ENCULTURATION. Enculturation is the process by which we learn how to function in life; the process by which culture itself is passed from generation to generation. Enculturation starts early in life with self-awareness, which allows individuals to assume personal responsibility for their conduct and to learn how to react and how to play various roles. Self-awareness gives one a positive view of self, motivating him to act to his advantage. In the process of enculturation, children gradually acquire a certain type of personality, which is actually the way a person thinks, feels, and behaves.[1] Personality is thus partially, at least, a product of enculturation. Nevertheless, personality formation takes place within genetic limitations, and it is shaped and enriched by unique experiences encountered during a lifetime. Consequent to the combination of these factors, no two persons are alike anywhere, and no two societies produce similar personalities. Yet, each society shares a number of common traits.

The purpose of this chapter is to analyze and explain the relationships between culture, behavior, and personality and to facilitate cross-cultural communication through the understanding of personality and national character.

Inside Personality

Scientists agree that personality formation starts early in life and is intense during the early years. They do not agree, however, to what degree personality is biologically inherited and to what degree it is learned through enculturation. Also, there is no consensus on whether mankind shares the same innermost traits. Based upon man's similar makeup and needs, some anthropologists advanced the idea of a "psychic unity" of all humans, claiming that "cultures produce divergent external trappings of customs and behavior while leaving the inner core of human experience untouched."[2] More recent research indicates that certain innate differences in personality are inherited, and other researchers speak of an "inner" and an "outer" personality, as well as of an even more external "role-playing" and "mask-wearing" personality (see figure 3-1).

The "inner" personality comprises our innermost desires, thoughts, fears, biases, superstitions, prejudices, aspirations, and dreams, which we only share with our closest friends and relatives, if we ever share them. At this level of interaction, we act informally and often add feelings and emotions to our thoughts and actions.

The "outer" personality refers to the behavior of any person in a larger social context from children interacting in school to the more formal behavior of adults in various social situations.

Eventually, certain social functions require a more rigidly prescribed social behavior as in diplomatic protocols, religious rituals, and selected governmental ceremonies. As such, this behavior does not represent the personality of the "role player," but rather the function being played out. Although such behavior is not part of everybody's personality in day-to-day life, certain cultures are known for being more formal and more ceremonial than others.

The "inner" personality changes very slowly, whereas the "outer" personality – especially the role-playing and mask-wearing ones – can change rather visibly. Nevertheless, between culture, behavior, and personality there is a mutual, subtle, and permanent relationship. Man is both the creator of culture and the product of culture. Strong personalities make profound impacts upon customs and behavior, and, in turn, culture shapes everyone's behavior and personality. Christianity started with one man and a handful of apostles, and it has reached into the behavior of hundreds of millions to touch everyone's personality. It is, however, a matter of debate whether or not in the end culture enters the "inner" personality to change the very nature of man. Such inner traits as fears, aspirations, or ideals are essentially shaped by the culture of a specific society. One may question, for example, how far 70 years of sustained ideological brainwashing has affected the inner personality of the Soviet citizens? This question would be difficult to answer, but the correlation between culture and behavior can be properly studied and addressed.

One can observe a variety of behaviors and personalities in any society, but some personality types will be more enduring and more frequent than others. This more common type will be the result of the proper behavior in a given environment, as well as of the entire experience of this particular culture. Such a representative personality is referred to as "modal" personality or national character, if it describes a nation. It is a statistical probability, but good enough as an approximation to allow researchers to use it in understanding ourselves and other cultures.

Analyzing the current enculturation in the United States, Dr. Massey, prominent American sociologist, distinguished several powerful sources that shape the personality of young Americans in different stages of formation.[3] To a certain degree, these sources are universal. The most important sources are:

- Family.

- Friends.

- School.

- Church (religion).

- Media (TV, especially in the United States).

Technology and geographic setting also play important roles in one's upbringing and behavior, and, as known, they differ from place to place and from society to society.

According to Dr. Massey, during their first years of life, children go through a period of intense "imprinting," where they are "programmed" to copy behavior and absorb values. Then, children go through a period of "modeling," where they imitate their heroes. Eventually, teenagers learn and assimilate values and behavior through "socialization," and gradually they start

LAYERS OF PERSONALITY

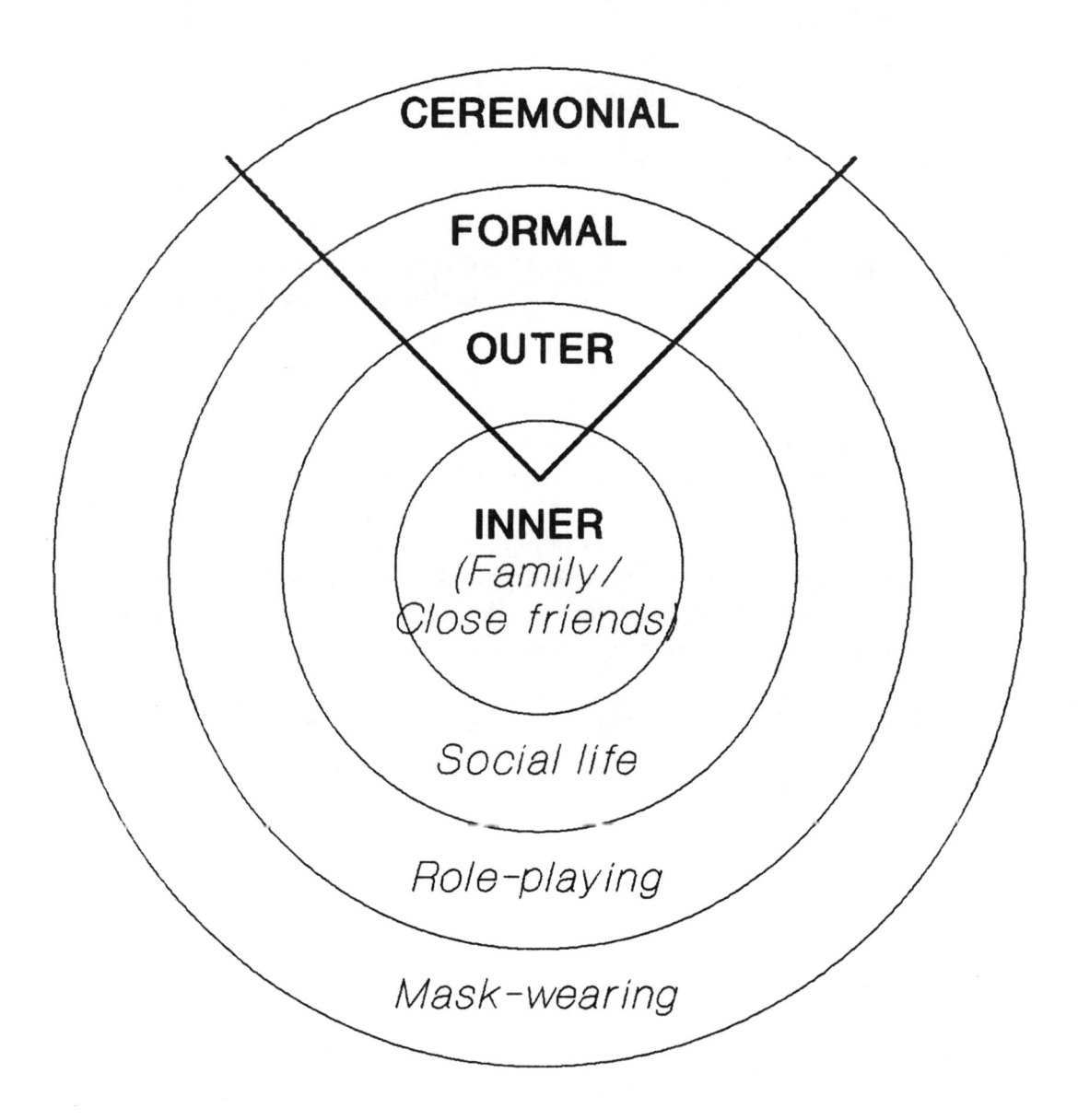

- CEREMONIAL
- FORMAL
- OUTER
- INNER *(Family/Close friends)*
- *Social life*
- *Role-playing*
- *Mask-wearing*

Figure 3-1

to challenge everything. By age 20, Dr. Massey continues, the personality is well shaped and values are solidly locked in everyone. From then on, only significant emotional events can influence and change one's behavior and personality.[4] Nevertheless, what is considered good behavior and normal personality in the United States is only typical for the American culture and may not be good or normal in another one. Such essential values are taught from childhood and remain rather constant throughout life for the same society. One can be shocked when confronted with the basic values and behavior of another culture.

Child rearing, for example, is supposed to be of instrumental importance in the process of enculturation and personality formation, but it differs greatly from culture to culture. In rural-agricultural societies with their extended families, child rearing is conducive to producing obedient, conformist, and compliant personalities. Such people generally perform routine agricultural work, stay in the same extended household where they conform to a prescribed structure, and very often work collectively. As adults, they are dependable and supportive of each other but have little private initiative and spirit of competitiveness.

By contrast, urban-industrial societies emphasize individual independence, self-reliance, and personal achievement. With fewer members in the family and with both parents working, children grow up with more freedom and limited personal attention or supervision. In addition, society at large and the school in particular will encourage competitiveness and will recognize and reward achievers for their success. However, excessive individualism can also breed aggressiveness and selfishness.

Interestingly, achievement, self-reliance, and independence were also encouraged and prized in preagricultural societies. By contrast with modern societies, however, such societies rewarded self-sacrificing individuals supportive of each other. Scientists have come to the conclusion that societies with centralized political authorities, such as the Communist countries where people are closely supervised, also produce obedient, conformist, and compliant personalities.[5]

As a result of enculturation, "normal" and "abnormal" become relative terms with little universal value. Even the most essential of all values – life itself – is open to interpretation. "Thou shalt not kill" becomes contextual and flexible from culture to culture. What is construed as murder in the Western World is justifiable homicide to this day in some remote areas of Amazonia. Accordingly, "moral" acts are all those acts that conform to certain cultural standards of good and evil in a given society at a given time, and each culture sets its own standards. Morality is definitely based on culturally determined ideals, and one author even observed sarcastically that it is normal to share the delusions traditionally accepted by your own society.[6]

This is not to say that essential values and beliefs, such as normal versus abnormal, good versus bad, or true versus untrue, are devoid of any meaning outside a given culture. If that were the case, mankind would still be in a savage state, there would be no point of reference, and communication across cultures would be almost impossible. Every culture has a basic sense of right and wrong that enables its members to survive. Religion even postulates that in the "inner" personality of man, or in our "common psyche," there is an innate sense of right and wrong that sets us apart from nature. According to religion, when man centered his life around the Creator, right was everything leading to pleasing God, to divine enlightenment, to attaining Nirvana, or to salvation. When man alienated himself from God and began to build a world around himself, the sense of right and wrong acquired a more relative meaning. Consequently, everything satisfying a certain society and its members became right and good, while the behavior and personality associated with doing what was expected as good became "normal."

From a religious point of view, normal and moral are universal values, and great religions, such as Christianity, have engaged in sustained efforts to moralize the world according to their tenets. From an anthropological point of view, however, the concept of normal behavior and normal personality assume full significance only within the limits of a specific culture. For example, in a society which encourages suspicion and aggression toward each other, the trusting and peaceful individual is considered abnormal. In another society where men are expected to be "macho," mild-mannered men will surely be considered weak and somehow abnormal.

As organic parts of culture, behavior and personality change steadily, but the pace of change is slow. Consequently, behavior remains characteristic for various societies for long periods of time, and predominant personality types endure. This in turn allows researchers and observers to discern the modal personality, which is typical for a society or a modern nation.

Generalizations do not always prove true in many cases, but most people still expect to find – and do find – a strong drive for personal achievement in the modal American personality, moderation in emotional expression in Japan, and, generally, modesty and reservation in the Far East. By properly understanding such personality types and the cultures which produced them, one can unravel the links between culture, behavior, and personality, and can communicate more efficiently across barriers. One should be fully aware, however, of ethnocentrism, stereotyping others, and judging them exclusively by one's own standards.

Ethnocentrism and Cultural Relativity[7]

Ethnocentrism refers to the unconscious tendency to view, judge, and interpret other people according to our own values. It is the tendency to place ourselves at the center of the world and rate all others accordingly. It is the unwarranted assumption that others will see the world as we see it. Although it can refer to various groups, it generally refers now to modern nations, and the bigger and more glorious the nations are, the deeper and more embedded their ethnocentric stand.

We all know, of course, that the United States is the greatest country on earth, but the British look down on everybody and truly believe that they are a superior people. For Frenchmen, however, France is the center of the entire universe, and its mission is to civilize the rest of us. Farther east, the Italians stand on top of the world; didn't Italy invent the Roman Empire? The Greeks have discovered everything from Alfa to Omega, and the Egyptians built pyramids before the Russians even existed as a nation. As for the Chinese, they are still the Middle Kingdom surrounded by barbarians on all sides. One can travel around the world many times without ever coming across people who are not ethnocentric.

On the positive side, ethnocentrism promotes cohesion among members of a nation and allows them to be satisfied and loyal members of their own society. On the negative side, ethnocentrism can easily lead to arrogance and aggressive behavior toward others. When politicized ethnocentrism is reinforced with religiocentrism and hardened by a sense of national mission, cross-cultural dialogue ceases. One can no longer see others objectively. And, if taken to the extreme, it can kill even the desire to communicate, thus becoming self-destructive. In many ways this is the current situation in the Middle East.

Ethnocentrism and the absolute values we tend to attribute to our own culture can also lead to stereotyping, misleading labeling, and empty prejudices. Stereotypes are hasty generalizations, and although they may contain considerable truth, they represent set attitudes through which we assign the same characteristics to all members of an ethnic group. Once a group is stereotyped, it is easy to label it and come to misleading conclusions. "All Indians in Latin America are short and stocky, and in the Andes they move so slowly that they must be lazy." When I visited South America, however, I was surprised to see that some of the Indians were rather tall. And then when I landed in La Paz, the thin air at that altitude exhausted me so quickly and made me move so slowly, that I became "lazier" than the Indians.

Stereotypes and false generalizations can blind us to the individual variations within a group and impede us from receiving new information. Consequently, in a cross-cultural communication context, we can send the wrong message or we can decode a message according to our preconceived ideas. This takes us to another element that blocks communication, which is prejudice.

Prejudice predisposes us to have a positive or negative attitude toward a person based solely on the membership of this person in a certain group – whether it be Mexicans, Blacks, "Russians" or, for that matter, Romanians. As a matter of fact, stereotypes and prejudices are related, and together they can put an end to meaningful communication. Instead of looking at a person and assessing his worth dispassionately, one can waste time looking for what reinforces one's preconceived expectations. Either way, favorably or unfavorably disposed, blind prejudice renders communication subjective and misleading.

The only way to escape this ethnocentric trap is by examining other cultures in a more detached and objective manner and by accepting that there is nothing wrong in being different. This does not mean that one has to embrace someone else's cultural stand, but it helps a lot to see others from a more neutral point of view. "Cultural relativism" will explain behavior, for example, from the point of view of the culture that has produced a personality. Once a behavior is placed in another environment, at a different level of technology where values and beliefs are different than ours, we can examine the behavior and personality of this particular culture for its own merits. Then, we can see where we stand; we can conclude if our values and beliefs are compatible or not, and afterward we can plan the best approach for communication.

One can analyze and understand a personality starting from the cultural milieu, or can understand the culture of a society starting from the behavior of its people. A good approach for understanding a culture is by examining its "modal" personality, but one should always remember that this is just a statistical generalization. It may not fit everyone, but as long as researchers remain objective and flexible, it is a good tool for understanding others and communicating with them.

Understanding "Modal" Personality

If one wants to understand, for example, the behavior of the Russian people, he can start from the physical environment and the history of Russia. The vastness, uniformity, and harshness of Russian lands did surely impact upon the behavior of the people. At the same time, the fact that historically Russia never experienced democracy in a Western sense would also reflect in the Russian behavior. One must also study the modal personality of the Russian in order to understand the culture behind it. Both of these approaches will enhance communication.

One special study of the Russian national character was completed after the Second World War and involved 3,000 refugees. A few hundred of those displaced people were specially investigated and 51 were studied in depth. What emerged from this study was a picture of the modal personality of the Russian people.[8]

The most pervasive Russian personality trait is affiliation, or a strong need to interact with others. Unlike average North Americans, Russians have little desire for personal achievement and low material expectations. They also display a certain need to depend on authorities, whom they expect to interfere with their lives. Consequently, Russians fear the authorities and expect little from them. Otherwise, in their daily lives, Russians rely heavily on a small and stable group of friends and are generally expressive, emotional, spontaneous, and gregarious.

Hedrick Smith, an American journalist who served several years as a correspondent in the Soviet Union in the seventies, wrote a remarkable book in which he described impressively the Russian character. Given the Soviet political environment, which is strongly conducive to conformism and suspicion, Smith observed a deep dichotomy between the "public" and "private" Russian (outer and inner personality), and, accordingly, the behavior is very different.

"So they adopt two different codes of behavior for their two lives – in one they are taciturn, hypocritical, careful, cagey, passive; in the other, they are voluble, honest, direct, open, passionate. In one, thoughts and feelings are held in check; in the other, emotions flow normally without moderation."[9]

To really know the Russians, Smith recommends, one should watch how they greet or part at a railroad station.

"They immerse each other in endless hugs, embraces, warm kisses on both cheeks, three times . . . firm kisses, often on the lips, and not only between men and women or between women, but man-to-man as well."[10]

And further the author writes: "This dichotomy of coldness and warmth springs in part from some deep duality of the Russian soul and temperament forged by climate and history. It makes the Russians, as a people, both stoics and romantics, both long-suffering martyrs and self-indulgent hedonists, both obedient and unruly, both stuffy and unassuming, both uncaring and kind, and both cruel and compassionate."[11]

Understanding the Russian modal personality and its dichotomy will help decipher and place behavior in one of the two modes. Then, mutual communication will be greatly enhanced.

If the Russian modal personality is obviously different than the American personality, then a Far Eastern one such as the Japanese modal personality is even more distant and more different. Unlike the argumentative Russians, the

Japanese appear to us to be extremely quiet. Most Americans hate silence, for example, and do not know what to do in a gathering or conference where nobody talks. Japanese, by contrast, can sit together for long periods without uttering a word and without feeling uncomfortable. Even in conferences, the Japanese can sit quietly and search for clues without saying anything. Most of the time, this causes Americans to feel very uncomfortable and makes them incorrectly believe that something is "wrong." The Japanese also hate to disagree and to contradict each other, or take a personal stand or make a decision alone. Generally, they come to a consensus among themselves and then take a stand and announce a decision. Such behavior puzzles and frustrates Americans doing business in Japan, who do not take the time to understand the intricate correlation between culture, behavior, and personality.[12]

If each national character, behavior, and personality is the result of its own environment and can best be understood in its own context, then, the most appropriate way to understand others and interact efficiently with them is by examining and understanding ourselves and our own culture.

ENDNOTES

1. William A. Haviland, *Cultural Anthropology* (New York: Holt, Rinehart and Winston, 1983), p. 139.
2. Juris G. Draguns, "Culture and Personality," in *Perspectives on Cross-Cultural Psychology*, edited by Anthony J. Marsella, Roland J. Tharp, and Thomas P. Ciborowski (New York: Academic Press, 1979), p. 179.
3. Morris Massey, *The People Puzzle* (Reston VA: Reston Publishing Co., 1979), pp. 25-51.
4. *Ibid*, pp. 18-20.
5. Haviland, pp. 144-5; and Gary R. Lee, *Family Structure and Interaction* (New York: J. B. Lippincott Co., 1977), p. 273.
6. Haviland, pp. 156-7.
7. Larry A. Samovar and Richard E. Porter, eds., *Intercultural Communications: A Reader*, 2nd ed. (Belmont, CA: Wardsworth Publishing Co., 1976), pp. 10-13.
8. Haviland, pp. 153-5.
9. Hedrick Smith, *The Russians* (New York: Ballantine Books, 1976), p. 140.
10. *Ibid*, p. 137.
11. *Ibid*, pp. 139-140.
12. L. Takeo Doi, "The Japanese Patterns of communication and the Concept of *Amae*," in Samovar and Porter, *Op. Cit.*, pp. 190-1.

Chapter 4
The American Modal Personality

Introduction

When dealing with people from other countries, we must be cognizant not only of the behavior, ideas, values, and attitudes at work in their cultures, but also of those contained within our own as well. Our cultural makeup will lead us to certain unconscious presumptions and prejudices. We need to be aware of those parts of our culture which are distinctly American and therefore different from others.

The United States, like any country, has a national character. There are obviously many points of divergence in this great melting pot of ours, but there are also many points on which we all converge as well. Despite the fact that Americans have come from all over the world and from every other culture, the United States is surprisingly homogeneous, much more so than most other countries. For a nation of our size and diversity, we have an amazing conformity in language, diet, hygiene, dress, basic skills, land use, community settlement, recreational activity, transportation and communications, and economic habits. This in turn reflects a rather small and consistent range of moral, political, economic and social values. Americans are not like anyone else on earth and our national character – our "modal personality" - reflects this uniqueness.

Geography has had a significant impact development on American culture. We have a country of continental dimensions stretching from the frozen tundra of Alaska to the tropical waters of the Caribbean and from the woodlands of New England to the islands of the South Pacific. Most of America is fertile and rich in resources. Moreover, the country has been and still is relatively thinly populated. Americans have generally felt that wealth was there for the taking, that there was plenty for anybody willing to work for it.

The people who first came to America have also left their imprint on our culture. Although many early Americans came over as indentured servants, and later as slaves, most people who have come to America over the years have come freely as free men, often to escape religious or political persecution in their home countries. The earliest American settlers brought with them rich Calvinist religion and ethical traditions and the Anglo-Saxon concepts of civil rights, the rule of law, and representative government. Those attitudes and values took on a peculiarly American hue as they evolved in the New World. Egalitarian democracy and secularism were part of the American cultural milieu by the 19th century. Though Americans have borrowed from virtually every other culture since then, these early tenets have remained the foundation of the American national character.

These political beliefs when combined with America's fortunate geographical situation gave rise to certain other cultural traits. The settlers and pioneers of the 17th to 19th centuries were faced with a hostile wilderness to be conquered and tamed. Everywhere they looked they saw problems to be solved, and solve them they did. Our predecessors had faith in mankind's ability to dominate the world around him, optimism about the future, and a belief in the inherent value of progress.

Man and Nature

Unlike many cultures which see men and nature as integral and equal parts of a whole, Americans tend to "see men" as separate from and superior to nature. We tend to view nature not in terms of aesthetics but in terms of utility. To us the natural environment is something to be conquered and improved upon. We cultivate and nurture those aspects of nature we find desirable. That which we deem undesirable, useless or bothersome, we eliminate. We have uprooted trees, cleared fields, exterminated species, leveled mountains, dammed rivers, drained lakes, and turned deserts into gardens. For most of our history, we have been profligate with our natural resources.

The American conquest and exploitation of the environment has been based on the belief that man is master. We assume that man can improve himself and the world around him. Our world is a rational one which can be explained and controlled. The cause of any particular occurrence can be determined. We then look to find a way to make it happen again if it is desirable or to prevent it from recurring if it is not.

Americans are empirical and pragmatic. As a rule, we are not prone to philosophical introspection. Most early Americans were not aristocrats or intellectuals. The majority of hem were middle or lower class who came here searching for a better material life. While today, the United States is second to none in academic or intellectual pursuits, the average American is much more action-oriented than idea-oriented. We are a nation of doers. Even the appellation "intellectual" is seen as slightly disparaging. Similarly, rarely do we find coherent, holistic personal philosophies or systematic ideologies among Americans. We are too practical for that. If an idea works, we use it, with little thought of the deeper philosophical implications of our actions.

This pragmatism is seen even in the American views on religion. We are largely a secular society and rarely mix religious ideas with secular ones. This does not mean that religion is not important. The Judeo-Christian ethic is deeply embedded in our culture so that even those Americans who profess atheism will support most of the teachings of the Judeo-Christian creed if taken out of their religious context. Americans are not anticlerical or antireligious, but we do tend toward a spirit of religious indifference. The majority of Americans do not concern themselves with religion in the conduct of most matters. More to the point, most of us, even those who hold deep religious convictions, at least implicitly believe that "God's will" is open to challenge. We retain responsibility for our lives and mastery of the world around us.

Optimism, the Future, and the Individual

American pragmatism implies an endemic optimism and faith in the effects of human effort. We are future oriented and generally believe that tomorrow will be better than today. To Americans, obstacles exist to be overcome. Adverse conditions need only be identified to be rectified. Whether it is space exploration, cancer research, or poverty, we are convinced that with unflinching effort and a "can-do" attitude, we can solve the problems. We have already put men on the moon, cured or eliminated deadly diseases, and created an affluent society. We are a healthy, prosperous, technologically advanced society with high rates of both consumption and production in a huge free mass market.

Most Americans believe that through hard work we can succeed at anything we want to do. There is no obstacle too great nor any goal too remote if we are just willing to make the effort. Accordingly, those who do not make it, the chronically poor or the unemployed, are seen as lazy or shiftless, bearing the consequences of their own actions, or rather their own lack of action. We have greater respect for the man who works for a subsistence wage than we do for one who draws welfare, even though the one on welfare may take home more money. The image of doing is dominant in American culture. To us, it is better to do something than to sit back and do nothing. This is quite a contrast to other cultures where men of high status may engage in meditation and contemplation, often making their livelihood by begging.

The idea that a person is responsible for his own destiny and is therefore responsible for his own success or failure is connected to the American view of the individual. We are a self-centered society. We see the individual as supreme. We tend to do what is best for ourselves, to maximize our own profit, pleasure, comfort, or well-being. We believe that if everyone is doing what is best for himself (within certain legal and moral boundaries) the society as a whole will benefit and improve. Even the State exists to see the individual rather than the other way around.

Implicit in our emphasis on the individual is the belief that everyone should have an equal opportunity and the freedom of choice to set and achieve his goals. We believe that people affected by a decision should have a hand in making that decision. Americans not only stand up for their fair share, but also generally expect that others will be treated fairly. This spirit of fairness and equality before the law has made the United States the most democratic society in the world. Most Americans find it difficult to understand the deliberate, ruthless exploitation that is common in many other cultures.

The American expectation of fairness can only be met in a society which tolerates differences among its members. The profusion of ethnic groups in the United States is conducive to this type of pluralism. Most Americans would agree at least in the abstract that discrimination should be eliminated, and we have made significant progress toward that goal. Similarly, Americans believe in cooperation and compromise to accomplish common goals. This does not mean we prostitute our values, only that we accept that the others have points of view which are entitled to our consideration.

American egalitarianism is also reflected in the informality of our inter-personal relations. We rely little on protocol or pomp and circumstance. It is not uncommon in the American workplace for employees to be on a first name basis with their bosses. In the military, it is common for soldiers of different grades to joke with one another. An officer who regularly "pulls rank" is viewed with disdain. Even our national leaders go to great pains to present themselves as one of the common folk, as men "of the people."

Since Americans believe that everyone should have an equal chance to achieve his life's goals, it is not surprising that we have developed an achievement-oriented culture. In our society, status is usually earned rather than inherited. Whereas people in other cultures will define themselves in terms of ascriptive qualities (*e.g.*, place of birth, family heritage, traditional status), an American's self-image is usually in terms of what he has achieved (*e.g.*, education, salary, position in a firm). The fulfillment of the individual is in material or social accomplishments which are personal, visible, and measurable. We proudly hang diplomas and citations on our walls. We judge books by the number of copies sold, athletes by points scored, and businessmen by dollars earned. Many Americans find the high status of the impoverished aristocrat or wandering religious ascetic in other cultures incomprehensible.

Americans especially like to display achievement through material goods. We like material well-being. We want, and feel we are entitled to, comfortable and convenient transportation, quick and reliable communications, clean and healthy food, nice homes with central heating and hot water, and labor-saving devices too numerous to count. We show others how much we have achieved in the houses we buy, the clothes we wear, and the cars we drive. Why will an American buy a car for $20,000 when one for half the price will meet his transportation needs? Because he can.

Progress, Time, and People

The American belief that nature is conquerable and our orientation toward the future give us a positive view toward progress. We see progress as fundamentally good and generally equate it with technological development. As a forward-looking society, we feel that the traditional way is not necessarily the best. We are constantly looking for new, better, more convenient ways to do things. Astounding technological advances such as computers, satellite communications, and organ transplants have been absorbed into our culture with scarcely a ripple.

Our striving for progress causes us to lead a fast-paced life. We are a kinetic society, always on the go. Even our vacations – the time we set aside for relaxation – are usually well planned and organized events wherein we cover great distances, see many places, and do several things in a relatively short period of time. Foreigners coming to America are often overwhelmed by the pace of American life, and they often perceive us as always being in a hurry (see figure 4-1). Conversely, many Americans overseas are frustrated by what they see as the lackadaisical attitude extant in foreign countries.

Our fast-paced lifestyle gives us a distinctive attitude regarding time. As a largely urban society, our lives are governed by the clock, not by the calendar or the daily fluctuations in temperature as in agrarian societies. We are extremely time conscious. We are punctual. Our activities are tightly scheduled and time is apportioned for separate activities. We hate to waste time or to be late. We even give distances in time units. Ask someone how far it is from Fort Bragg to Washington, D.C., and the odds are he will say "5 to 6 hours" instead of "300 miles."

Our time orientation causes us to make a clear distinction between work and play. To Americans "time is money" and we forego play or leisure to work. Work is something we do for a living. It is regular, purposeful, guided. Play is relief from the drudge and regularity of work. It is enjoyable in its own right. Many Americans of course do enjoy their work, but this is usually seen as a happy coincidence and is secondary to doing the job. Nor does "play" necessarily mean that we exert less effort. Many Americans play with as much or more intensity as they work. Moreover, much of what we do for recreation, such as physical exercise, gardening, or woodworking, is seen as work elsewhere. In many cultures, there is no clear dichotomy between work and play. Often the time of the most important work is the time of the greatest festivity, such as planting or harvest season.

Some non-Western cultures take work casually. Any employer who attempts to pay an hourly wage is likely to find that an inordinate amount of time is used to accomplish tasks that are done quickly by American workers paid by the hour. Many countries even set aside substantial blocks of time in the

TO OTHERS, AMERICANS ALWAYS APPEAR TO BE IN A HURRY.

Figure 4-1

middle of the workday for rest. Similarly, meetings rarely convene or adjourn on time. Many foreigners see business meetings as a sort of social gathering and will spend a great deal of time making small talk.

Americans see this as a waste of time and prefer a more direct, impersonal approach. Since we are achievement oriented, we are impatient with whatever impedes efficiency in accomplishing our goal. We want to get down to business, stay to the point in negotiations, make decisions, get results. Foreigners often find this brash and overbearing. This is epitomized in a story about an American engineer working in the Middle East. When he complained to his Arab counterparts about the lack of progress in negotiations, he was politely told, "Rome was not built in a day." "That's because they didn't have an American foreman," responded the American. He reportedly lost the contract.

The peripatetic nature of the American lifestyle has not only made an impact on our business relationships but also on our more personal relationships. The high degree of geographic and social mobility in our society makes lifelong friendships difficult. Americans are quite friendly and like to be liked. In fact, we place great value on being accepted, and are sensitive to praise and criticism. But while we tend to have numerous personal relationships, very few of these are deep and long lasting. We quickly make new friends when we change status or locale and almost as quickly lose contact with our old ones. Americans are hard to get to know intimately. We tend to eschew personal commitments or lasting social obligations.

This lack of strong personal ties carries over into American family life. Unlike other cultures, where the joint extended family is dominant, we tend to have weak family links. It is not unusual for adult siblings to go for several years without seeing one another. Rarely will an American have strong vertical or horizontal family ties outside the nuclear family. Even this basic kinship unit may be phasing out of our culture. The number of working women and single-parent households have both increased substantially in recent years so that nuclear family ties are becoming weaker. American children are encouraged at progressively earlier ages to become independent and fend for themselves in many ways. Similarly, elderly people are often required to live by themselves or in retirement houses rather than relying on their children for support. Unlike other cultures where the family respects and cares for the aged, our elderly are often shunted aside.

Conclusion

We see then that Americans are pragmatic, rational, energetic, optimistic, egalitarian, informal, achievement-oriented, materialistic, progressive, time-conscious, independent, and friendly but not intimate. These cultural traits have contributed to a high level of technological development, affluence, and greatness in the international arena. They have also contributed to high rates of illegal drug use, broken families, and ulcers. In and of themselves, these traits are neither good nor bad. It is simply the way we are. We are different from other people because our environment and our history are different. We owe no apologies for that, nor should we attempt to change ourselves to meet the expectations of people in other cultures. That is not only undesirable, but also it is impossible. But, we can and should be aware of what it is that makes us culturally American and of the intellectual baggage we carry with us as a result. Such an awareness will make us more effective in cross-cultural communications. It will probably make us better Americans as well.

ENDNOTES

For further information, see L. Robert Kohls, *Survival Kit for Overseas Living* (Yarmouth, Maine: Intercultural Press, Inc., 1984); and Edward C. Stewart, *American Cultural Patterns: A Cross-Cultural Perspective* (Pittsburgh: University of Pittsburgh, 1974).

Chapter 5
Culture Shock And Cultural Adjustment

Introduction

People who live most of their lives in a small place may be shocked by the hectic life of a big city. It may take a long time to adjust to the new pace of life, and some people may never fully become part of the new place. However, when one is assigned to work abroad in a completely different culture, the move can really be shocking. The immediate result for an inexperienced and unprepared person could be disorientation, confusion, and even mental depression. The syndrome was diagnosed and identified by the anthropologist Kalvero Oberg as "culture shock."[1]

According to Oberg, culture shock begins with the anxiety that results from changing our familiar cultural environment and losing all the signs and symbols of one's native social milieu. These include thousands of signs and cues by which we orient ourselves daily – from greeting and shaking hands to accepting or rejecting invitations and when to take statements seriously or not. They also include little cues such as gestures, facial expressions, customs, and norms which everyone is enculturated with without being aware of it. One's peace of mind and work efficiency depend to a high degree on all these daily signs and cues to which one pays little or no conscious attention. These cues become "normal" and people take them for granted, expecting them to be universal. One actually becomes aware of them only by losing them, when he or she moves to a new culture where things are different. Culture shock is experienced by many Americans working abroad and by foreigners or immigrants coming to the United States.

Most native Americans, for example, are unaware of how difficult it is for a foreigner with a limited knowledge of English and American culture to grasp the full meaning, nuance, and usage of such common greetings as Hi! Hello! How are you? How do you do? What are you doing? What's up? How's it going? What's going on? What's happening? Hey man! and so on. Occasionally, people who are not familiar with the idiomatic meaning of such expressions are tempted to answer with a full explanation rather than another symbolical expression. Eventually, people will learn the greetings, but there are numerous cues that are unique to a particular culture, which will not be found in other cultures.

Culture shock is the total effect upon a person of a new physical and cultural environment where people behave differently, speak another language, use different signs and symbols, and have other values and beliefs. Culture shock is exacerbated when the difference between the American culture and the new culture is big, when the experience and resilience of the person assigned to the new country are limited, and when one has little knowledge of the new country and has high, unrealistic expectations of it.

According to Robert Kohls, the most common symptoms of culture shock are homesickness, boredom, withdrawal, fatigue, compulsive eating and drinking, irritability, exaggerated preoccupation with cleanliness, excessive fear (of being robbed for example), family tension, hostility toward local nationals, and, eventually, the inability to work efficiently. Although culture shock is started by anxiety and frustration caused by what appears to be an "ambiguous" environment, it is completely different from normal frustration. As a matter of fact, culture shock starts gradually, without a specific cause or a clear beginning, and it builds up slowly. It has a cumulative effect and in the end it can even result in physical illness.

Most researchers have concluded that there are four stages in the adjustment of a person assigned to work abroad. Depending on their personal ability and motivation, most individuals go through these stages, but the length and depth of each stage varies from person to person. The four stages are:

- A short period of euphoria.

- A period of irritation and hostility.

- A period of gradual adjustment.

- The final adaptation.

During the first stage, which can vary from some two weeks to about two months or so, most people feel like "tourists." They are fascinated by the new place. They focus upon the pleasant side and conclude that after all, people are similar everywhere, and they like it. If they don't stay overseas too long they retain beautiful recollections as most tourists do. However, if they stay long enough, the culture shock is almost inevitable. Interestingly, there are people who love the new country in the beginning and end up hating it later, and others who hate it in the beginning and grow to like it later.

Gradually, one's attention shifts from similarities and beautiful things to differences and ugly things, which exist side by side everywhere in the world. Some of the problems that one has to put up with after the "honeymoon" period – such as poor public transportation, dirty streets, or low standards of living – are real, but they come with the new country and there is not much one can do about them. Women in particular will encounter more frustration and obstacles, because most of the world does not treat them on an equal par with men. Many Americans are also shocked by the political reality of other countries such as repressive regimes and lack of freedom, as well as by various exotic religions for which they have no understanding. Other problems, nevertheless, are in the mind and attitude of the beholder, and they can be changed. Unfortunately, at this stage most people start to compare everything to the "American Way," and worse still, they usually remember the best things at home and compare them with the worst ones abroad.

One of my most shocking experiences was during my first train trip in India, which was from Calcutta to Benares. It was an overnight journey which lasted 24 hours instead of the normal 12 hours. As advised, I had reserved a first-class, sleeping couch ticket, and expected to sleep well while on my way to the Holy City. The first shock came when I eventually found my car and my compartment, where someone was already sleeping on my couch. The conductor – whom I only saw at the beginning of the trip – evicted the man from my "bed," and then smiled and wished me a good night. Actually, I did not sleep at all the whole night. What I had expected was an European-type sleeping car with a regular bed, clean sheets, a pillow and a blanket, an attendant, and a pleasant hotel-like atmosphere; but such things only existed in my mind. In reality, I was locked up in a dirty, stinky, moving iron box, and I was lying on a wooden bench which was covered by a piece of dusty plastic. There were no sheets, no pillow, no blanket, no attendants – just the smoke and dust entering from outside. The next day, the train assumed the schedule of a slow-moving passenger train full of local peasants traveling a few miles, who were incapable of speaking any English. The train was not on its regular schedule, I could not figure out where I was, and the conductor was nowhere to be found. As the second night approached I tried to find the conductor, but to my dismay I realized that there was no way to go from one car to another as each one was completely blocked from the others. Being afraid to consume local food, I did not dare touch anything offered by occasional vendors in various railroad stations. With night approaching, I grew even more worried and I nearly panicked when, with great difficulty, I understood that the train would not go to Benares but to a railroad junction a good distance away. I simply felt like a prisoner of a moving train advancing nowhere in the dark of night. Finally, a friendly and smiling Indian took me to the bus station in Mughal Saray and accompanied me to Benares, and I felt like I was regaining my freedom and confidence. The Gautam Hotel in downtown Benares seemed like a little paradise. While on the train, I wanted to blame all the Indians and to curse their railroads. But in a clean bathtub with hot water, I slowly changed my mind. I even remembered the awful impression that the Bronx made upon a friend of mine who came from Sweden to visit me in New York. He could not believe with his own eyes that such a neighborhood existed in the richest country in the world. One cannot judge America by the Bronx or India by a railroad journey. Nevertheless, such experiences build frustration and cause aggressiveness toward the host country.

Usually, inexperienced Americans try to take refuge in the diplomatic community after such encounters in a new country. They may resort to unwarranted derogatory remarks about the host culture, and may isolate themselves from the local people. This is a crucial stage in the process of adjustment – the stage where people need help to overcome both the real difficulties and their own attitude, and the sooner they overcome them the sooner they will start to function normally.

From Shock to Adaptation

Adjustment comes gradually with patience, with more understanding toward the host culture and the behavior of the people, and with linguistic proficiency. Slowly but surely, one becomes more comfortable and regains his confidence, goodwill, and humor. At some point, one can even make fun of such encounters and can offer help to the newcomers undergoing the same process of uneasy transition. In a way, helping others is helping oneself, and once being capable of offering help, one is virtually well on his way to accepting the new culture and being able to function in the new society.

During the last and final stage of adjustment, one has become bicultural in a way, being not only completely capable of understanding the new culture, but to also work in it as well. Somehow, one develops a third personality capable of operating each of the two cultures and between the two of them. The problems have not been eliminated, but they are sorted out and treated accordingly. One learns, for example, how to cope with a poor transportation system, what to do about occasional power shortages, where to eat out, how to treat the local people, and so on. At the same time, one also learns that the behavior, values, and beliefs of a society do not change easily, and that what can be changed without much risk is one's own attitude toward diversity. The outcome is enriched personal experience, more confidence, and biculturalism with all its rewards.

Kohls also observed that during the sojourn of a person overseas, there are actually two cycles of culture shock which accommodate themselves to the amount of time one stays abroad. He also warned that sometimes the second cycle is even more severe than the first one. It makes a big difference, however, if one knows that the culture shock is nothing abnormal or not an illness, but simply symptoms associated with changing one's cultural environment. The sooner one identifies and diagnoses the symptoms, the better his chances are of overcoming them. Here are a few steps that you should take to minimize the effects of culture shock:

- Learn everything possible about the country of assignment.

- As much as possible, learn the language of the country and remember that even a little is a lot more than nothing.

- Sort out problems and try to solve those that can be solved.

- Avoid the company of those who have failed to adjust to the new culture.

- Establish a good local contact with a sympathetic attitude and seek out his assistance.

- Remember that the assignment is for a limited period of time, and the purpose is successful performance.

Eventually, if one stays long enough overseas and integrates himself well in the host country, he may even like it very much and encounter problems of reintegration upon returning to the United States. In fact, America may change, too, after a few years. There may be new words and new expressions in the vocabulary, new stores in the neighborhood, and new gadgets on the market. There may be more traffic congestion, and the people may have formed new habits and attitudes. The Americans may now appear cool and distant, always in a hurry, and always trying to do something or to achieve something. If this is the case, one already sees them through the eyes of another culture acquired while stationed abroad. Consequently, one can encounter the culture shock in reverse, which is again normal and of which one is not normally aware. Geography makes different cultures, and history changes each of them. When one grows and changes with a culture, one is not usually aware of the change, and everything appears "normal."

ENDNOTES

1. Quoted in L. Robert Kohls, *Survival Kit for Overseas Living* (Yarmouth, Maine: Intercultural Press Inc., 1984), Chapter 18.

CHAPTER 6
VERBAL AND NONVERBAL COMMUNICATION

Introduction

The purpose of this chapter is to explain how people communicate within any culture, to analyze the link between language and culture, and to facilitate better verbal and nonverbal cross-cultural communication.

As behavior, communication is an intrinsic part of any culture. Human culture is such that one must be able to communicate. Alongside language and behavior, communication evolved from the simple ways of primitive communities to the highly sophisticated ways of communication of the modern world. At the same time, it evolved from transmitting simple ideas related to the physical world to the transmission of highly abstract values, beliefs, and concepts. Such abstractions exist only in the minds of people of similar culture and background. In the process, man grew wiser, more knowledgeable, and more complex.

Communication embraces a variety of forms – from the organization of space around us and the way a society interacts with its physical environment to the abstract form of verbal interaction. As expected, communication among members of the same culture, sharing a similar environment and speaking the same language, is easier than cross-cultural communication. Furthermore, the more distant two cultures are and the more different their languages, the more difficult it is to communicate.

Most scholars agree that the spoken language is an extremely important medium of expression and communication. However, while being considered the greatest invention of man, language could equally be an instrument of understanding and misunderstanding. Moreover, it has been estimated that only about 30 percent of average interpersonal communication is transmitted through the spoken word. The other 70 percent is equally divided between para-language and body language. In addition, we communicate through the organization of space around us, through our place in it, and through our orientation in time.

While it is universally acknowledged that what people say on various occasions is very important, it should also be stressed that the overall impression people make is even more important in the process of communication. For instance, a leading American politician visited a Latin American country. Wherever he went he said the right things, yet his choices of places to visit and his body language and signs communicated the wrong messages. Among other things, when the journalists asked him at the airport how his flight was, he answered that it was just perfect and flashed the typical American sign for "OK." The picture with this emblem appeared on the front page of a leading local newspaper, but the sign is a very obscene gesture in this particular country. Several such mistakes ruined the trip. In cross-cultural communication, language must be used in its proper cultural context and in conjunction with adequate para-language and kinesics.[1]

Language, Culture, and Communication

Between culture and language there is an intricate relationship, and proper communication requires a good understanding of the culture behind the language. As an essential part of culture, language has evolved along with man and has equally influenced and reflected his culture. Knowing another language is of instrumental importance for good communication as long as we know that vis-a-vis culture, language is like the tip of an iceberg. What is visible and apparently easy to understand is only a fraction of the invisible part beneath the water. The visible (audible) language expresses the invisible culture and thoughts, and, in turn, thoughts are shaped by the language.

It has been estimated that presently there are about 3,000 spoken languages in the world and a lot more local dialects. Some of these languages are used by a small group of people, while others are spoken by hundreds of millions. They reflect the civilization of man in all its stages and, according to the needs and level of evolution of various cultures, the size of these languages vary from a few thousand words to hundreds of thousands. Furthermore, the lexicon or vocabulary is only one element of the language. Knowing words is important, but knowing how to use them is even more important.

According to their vocabulary, languages have been divided between rich, medium, and poor. English is the richest language in the world, and its vocabulary has been estimated at about 750,000 words. French is the next richest language and employs some half a million words. Medium languages have about 200,000 to 300,000 words, and poorly developed languages have under 50,000 words. Some little developed or vanishing languages could have even fewer words.[2]

Within the same language, people know and use a limited number of words depending on their education and specialization. King James' Bible, printed in 1610, was written with only 6,000 words, and it served its purpose well. Shakespeare used 34,000 words in his writings, and he is considered the "richest" English author. By comparison, good writers of today use only about 15,000 to 20,000 words, and regular speakers of English go throughout a lifetime employing a great deal fewer words.[3] Scientists have established that there are over 30 million species of animals on earth. How well do we know our physical world, and how well can we express it? Can we know everything, or do various cultures and societies have to know everything to function well?

When the horse provided the chief means of transportation in the United States, there were thousands of words associated with the harnessing of horses and the use of carriages. Now, not only are there thousands of new words associated with the automobile industry, but also a whole new "computerese" language. People in the tropics use thousands of words to describe palm trees, and so do people in the deserts to describe their camels. In how many words can a German describe a palm tree or a camel? How many words do they use in North Carolina to describe snow? For the same snow, Eskimos have over 30 words and Amazonian Indians have none. How can we expect to communicate properly in such a linguistic "chaos"? One can legitimately ask then, What is a language and what is its place in culture and communication? In a strict sense, language is a set of symbols (words), and a set of rules (grammar and syntax) for their use. The meaning of the symbols, however, is peculiar only to a given culture and even to a particular group of people using them. The grammar and syntax also vary extensively, particularly from one linguistic family to another. In some American Indian languages, for example, there are no past or future tenses, per se, and the tense of the action must come from the context. In a broad sense, "language is the symbolic representation of a people, and it includes the historical and cultural background as well as their approach to life and their ways of living and thinking."[4] Each language develops in a given culture to serve its members. What and how it is represented is very much a function of culture. Thus, language and culture are inseparable, and good communication requires a good understanding of both. Only mathematics, as a further refined symbolization, can provide us with a more universal language, but such a "language" would be understood by very few people.

All over the world, languages report information and shape perceptions of reality. They enhance our ability to reason, to argue logically, and to explore and understand the world and ourselves. Yet, no two societies do it the same way, because their environments, needs, inclinations, and experiences are different. Words are also symbols of reality, not reality itself, and the full meaning of symbols cannot be completely understood outside its culture even when apparently it refers to the same notion. Even a simple and well-defined thing of the real world can be treated differently in two different languages. Spanish for example, has only one word, "dedo," for a "finger" or a "toe," but it has two words for "you."

We need to understand and organize the otherwise chaotic universe around us. Accordingly, we give labels to portions of the continuous physical environment, but depending on our culture, not everything is of equal importance. Consequently, the arctic landscape is a lot better understood and described by its inhabitants, and so is the tropical environment by its population. The result is that people perceive reality differently, and what might be an objective reality existing by itself outside, assumes various subjective shapes in our minds. This hypothesis was first formulated by Whorf: "Each language embodies and perpetuates a particular world-view. The speakers of a language agree to perceive and think of the world in a certain way, but not in the only possible way."[5] No language provides a label (word) for everything, and many words or expressions must be explained rather than translated. If a particular culture does not have a word for a certain color, for example, this color must be explained. And usually, if there is no word for a color in a given culture, this culture does not recognize it; therefore, this color does not exist for its members. In the Navajo language, for example, there is only one word for green and blue, and the differences in tint must be explained.[6]

Languages are also dynamic and, as culture itself, they change steadily. Linguists have estimated that the basic vocabulary changes very slowly, but many words and expressions with their annotations and connotations change rather quickly. From this point of view, basic words referring to the physical environment and daily activities, which have a more precise annotation, are easier to translate and understand cross-culturally. A "dog," for instance, is a dog all over the world, although dogs come in thousands of shapes, sizes, and colors. "Animal" is already a more abstract category. Translating the word is easy, but some people may not be willing to place birds or insects along with animals. And the distinction between plants and animals can also be blurred in the world of microorganisms.

Nouns can be translated easily if we find the right equivalent. Verbs are already more difficult because they vary with grammar, and grammar is so different from language to language. Adjectives bring us into the connotative world of values, but here, "beauty is in the eye of the beholder." The connotative meaning of words also involves a personal attitude and an evaluative dimension such as positive, neutral, or negative. And as everyone knows, it is not easy to be part of a culture and be neutral about it. "Nepotism," for example, is a well-known concept, but not all Americans know that its root "nepot" means grandson in Latin. This bit of information should clarify its meaning, but how should the concept be translated into a non-European language?

In Chinese, for example, the pictographic representation of the English word "good" is a woman and child (son). Obviously, the man who "possessed" them had something good, which, in turn, tells us about the male-dominated values of the Chinese culture. And as we move farther up in the cultural "pyramid," the meaning of words and expressions is increasingly connotative, and its simple translation is no longer possible. Cross-cultural communication is further complicated by the usage of restricted verbal codes such as jargon and abbreviations. They are generally understood only by the members of a group or a subculture where a good part of the intended message is already known.

When mastering a foreign language, certain differences of meaning can be understood easily and bridged. In a traditional African village, for example, "brother" means not only the sons of the same parents, but also all of the young men in the village. In the Balkans, an "uncle" or "aunt" is every man or woman in the village who is old enough to be an uncle or an aunt. In Russia, every woman who is old enough to be a grandmother is referred to as a "babushka." "Friend" means a lot more in many developing countries than in the United States. "Love" is vaguely defined in various countries. "Democracy" is interpreted totally differently in France and Korea. Nevertheless, there are certain equivalents for these words, but how can one translate "Karma" in English, "Islamic Jihad" in Spanish, and "Immaculate Conception" in Urdu? Thinking of my cross-cultural classes, it made me laugh when I heard a televangelist saying that we need a strong dose of "Biblical diet." How would I translate this concept in Nepali?

The concept of religion is very abstract, and it means various things in different parts of the world. In most European languages, religion comes from "religare," which in Latin means tying again or tying back (impliedly) to God. The Arab equivalent is "diin," which when translated means a group of people who believe in God. The Chinese equivalent is "zong jiao," which in direct translation is the teachings of the ancestors. Are we sure that we all mean the same thing?[7]

If mastering a language is very important, understanding the culture behind it is essential. And skillful linguistic communication also requires an adequate knowledge of nonverbal cues. Such cues include paralanguage or the use of sounds and silence, kinesics or body languages, the proper use of space and place, and others which may equally enhance or impede communication.

To an outsider an unknown language can sound from beautiful to ugly, from soft to aggressive, and from incoherent to musical. Words may appear to be lumped together in a confusing way and, occasionally, sounds by themselves may sound "dirty" and could trigger undesirable notions in the mind of the listener. When one understands the "sound" equivalent of a word that might be dirty in another language, inasmuch as possible, such a word should be avoided.

Languages also vary with the area, with the social class and occupation of the speakers, and with the sex and age of both speakers and listeners. In addition, some languages are more flowery, rhetorical, and even hyperbolical, while others appear to be more factual and more concise. Romance-root languages such as Spanish, for example, employ more terms of endearment than others. A TV announcer may start his presentation by saying: "Dear telespectators, it is a great privilege and an honor to be able to address you..." Threatening and strong language is more readily accepted among Russians, who even wonder why we take offense at such trivial verbal abuse. The proper perception of a language is in the ears and minds of those who have created it. Otherwise, there is in every language a polite and impolite way to express oneself, as well as a proper and improper way of usage.

Paralanguage and Body Language[8]

It is said that it is easy to lie with words, more difficult to lie with the face, and even more difficult to do so with the body. And if the spoken words relay only part of the message, a good part of it is expressed through various other sounds and the entire body. A good synchronization of speech and movement, used properly in the cultural context, will give any speaker enhanced credibility.

Paralanguage refers to the sound, noise, pause, speech rate, pitch of voice, volume, tone, inflection, modulation, accent and accentuation, as well as silence, suspense, and pause a person may use to enhance and direct his communication. The simple expression "Oh Yes," for example, may be uttered to express a whole array of attitudes. Paralanguage can add a great deal of feelings and credibility to the otherwise dry verbal expression.

Pause, silence, and suspense can also be masterfully used by people and actors. The renowned Soviet comedian A. Raikyn once appeared on a scene alone, took a chair, and sat and sat and sat without uttering a word. It was during the sixties after the de-Stalinization period. After a short period of total silence, the spectators began to feel uneasy and to whisper in surprise. "What is the matter with you?" the actor asked the audience. "You cannot be quiet for two minutes? I sat like that for three years!"

Body language refers to facial expressions, gestures, position, and movement, and their relation to communication. They differ greatly from culture to culture and there is no dictionary to translate them.

American society is rather "horizontal." People are presumed equal and are treated democratically. They are taught from childhood to stand up for their beliefs, to look others in the eyes, to have the courage to defend their positions, and to say yes or no. Most of the countries of the world are rather "vertically" stratified, and an indiscriminate American stand could easily be construed as rude and may block communication.

Facial expressions such as smiles, frowns, winking, and yawns can have enormous consequences. Eye contact alone can carry and miscarry a lot of information, and it is more typical of the Western World. Staring at strangers is impolite. Extended eye contact is rude. Avoiding eye contact can be a sign of insecurity. Shifty eyes could diminish the credibility of one's words or could be interpreted as hiding something. In many countries, such as Japan, for example, younger people do not stare at an older person, or if they do so they must be the first to lower their eyes. While attending a lecture, it is all right for the students to follow the teacher, but it is not acceptable for a lecturer to look fixedly at the same person throughout the presentation.

Facial expressions also vary with the culture. Americans smile more often than the more cynical Europeans. After all, what's there to smile about after two devastating wars? Buddhist people, trained to resign earthy pleasures, smile even less than the Europeans. The Japanese, who are trained to be stoic and to hide their anguish, might even smile in situations in which an American will cry. One important element of the culture shock is the fact that when changing cultures, we are no longer capable of "reading" the new faces. People appear to smile permanently in a phony way, or to wear an "unexplainable" straight face. Under such conditions, a simple eyebrow flash or an innocent but prolonged stare may send an unintended message. On other occasions, some Americans, conditioned by the superior US technology and high standard of living, may have a patronizing look or a condescending smile, which will be equally rejected. Diffusing the tension caused by any one of these expressions will not be easy.

Body posture and stance communicate a lot, also. Standing while a superior or an older person is "talking" to you is common in the Far East. Sitting side by side with your chief while in his office is common in the American society. Remember, however, that most of the world is not equalitarian. Treating everybody as equal in India, for example, will make you only equal to the lowest caste. Slouching in a chair, which is so typical of American students, is considered rude in many parts of the world. Putting your feet on a desk and showing the soles of the shoes is taken as an insult in almost any country.

There are body contact and non-contact societies. Most Americans do not like to touch much, especially within the same sex group. They also shake hands less than others, such as Europeans. From the body touch point of view, cultures vary widely. The Chinese almost never touch or kiss in public. The Arabs touch and kiss quite a lot, but within the same sex. It is pretty common to see Arab men walking hand in hand, without any sexual connotation. By comparison with others, the Russians prefer a strong handshake. Handshaking has been recently introduced to the Far East and can create confusion when it is used alongside the traditional bow. Handshaking is prolonged sometimes for the entire conversation in Black Africa, causing most Americans to feel very uneasy about it to the point of not being able to carry on a discussion. Shaking hands with a woman, or even worse, kissing her hand in the old European fashion, would be an enormous blunder in the Middle East. And the "dictionary" of body languages can go on forever.

Physical attitude, walking, signs, and gestures are also common communicators. The hasty pace of life in New York makes everybody rush as if there will be no tomorrow. By contrast, in some small cities in Latin America, people walk as if nothing would have to be done until "manana." An Army officer remarked that the South Koreans do not smoke in front of their superiors, and if they do so, they smoke as if they were ashamed of it and would like to hide it. By contrast, an American prisoner of war who had escaped from a German camp during the Second World War was apprehended in a railroad station. He was identified by the way he walked around, he sat, and he smoked.

Hand signs, gestures, and emblems translate extremely poorly, and unless their meaning is known they should not be used (see figure 6-1). For instance, we know that the OK sign is obscene in Latin America; however, the hitchhiking sign is scornful in the Middle East. Perception and meaning reside in the perceiver and his culture. The "V" (victory) sign is unknown in most of the world, and such emblems as the Swastika, David's Star, the Semi-crescent, and the Communist Red Star only have significance for those who have come into contact with them. Nevertheless, using such symbols indiscriminately in the wrong place can be ruinous.

Superstition is also universal. One should not extend a hand with the fingers spread toward a person in Greece because it means "the five curses." Looking persistently at somebody in the Middle East can be perceived as "the evil eye," and to protect themselves people wear special amulets. Patting a child on the head is abhorred in the Far East, because in the popular beliefs of some people that gesture could stop the growth of the child. Of course, the Americans are not superstitious; however, they knock on wood to drive away evil spirits, and they eliminate the 13th floor in high-rises. While certain cultures hide their superstitions, others are open about them. The Chinese, for example, would not sit 13 people around a table.

Many times, what we say will be forgotten. What will be remembered will be the total projection, and in the end others will perceive us not necessarily as we are, but as we act – such as strong, open, friendly, reliable, or otherwise. It is also important to make a good first impression, because we will never have a second chance to make it. However, there are exceptions to any rule. It is alleged that shortly after his arrival to the United States, Einstein was invited to address a select group of American academics and the scientist showed up neglectfully dressed. "Sir," one of his aides told him, "you are an important person, you should dress accordingly." And Einstein replied, "Why? Nobody knows me anyway." Years later when he was a celebrity, Einstein was asked to address the group again, and again he showed up carelessly dressed. "Sir, these people know you. You should dress elegantly," the same aide told the scientist. But Einstein replied calmly, "What's the reason? They know who I am anyhow." There are few Einsteins in this world, however, and most of us must prepare carefully for good communication.

Space, Place, and Other Communicators

From an unending list of nonverbal communicators, the organization and use of space and man's spatial relations (proxemics) are probably the most visible. As part of the physical environment, space is a finite commodity and not always available. Nevertheless, man does not have a strong sense of "territoriality," and except for the psychological fear of open spaces (agoraphobia) and enclosed spaces (claustrophobia), which can afflict individuals everywhere, man's spatial relations are culturally determined.

A group of primitive people, for example, living in a jungle at a preagricultural level, would blend themselves so well with nature, that in many ways they would appear to be part of it. On the other hand, agricultural fields can be neat and elaborate, and when seen from an airplane, they may look like beautiful abstract paintings. Further up on the technological scale, industrial societies can improve the space around us, but they can also damage the environment and can make life ugly and unhealthy.

People are creators and products of culture. They shape the environment and the surrounding space, and they are shaped by the environment. They grow and change with it, and if the balance between man and nature is harmonious, each society assumes that its spatial relations are just "normal." Only when visiting other countries do we start to realize that some of our assumptions were conditioned by our upbringing. For most Americans, for example, and particularly so for those who grew up in the sparsely populated Midwest, European cities have too many people, and East Asia is unacceptably crowded. To a European eye, a lot of land is "wasted" everywhere in the United States. To an American eye, European land is overused and farming looks more like gardening. After 20 years of American enculturation, I also began to see Europe through the American culture. Approaching Munich by train, for example, I was more than surprised to see that every little plot of land in the immediate vicinity of the train rails was used for some gardening. Such a thing is unimaginable in the United States. Then, when I took a shower in a Geneva hotel, I hit a wall with every move of my body as if the shower room had 10 walls instead of 4. It became obvious to me that Europe has far less space than we do.

CERTAIN SIGNS AND GESTURES SHOULD BE AVOIDED.

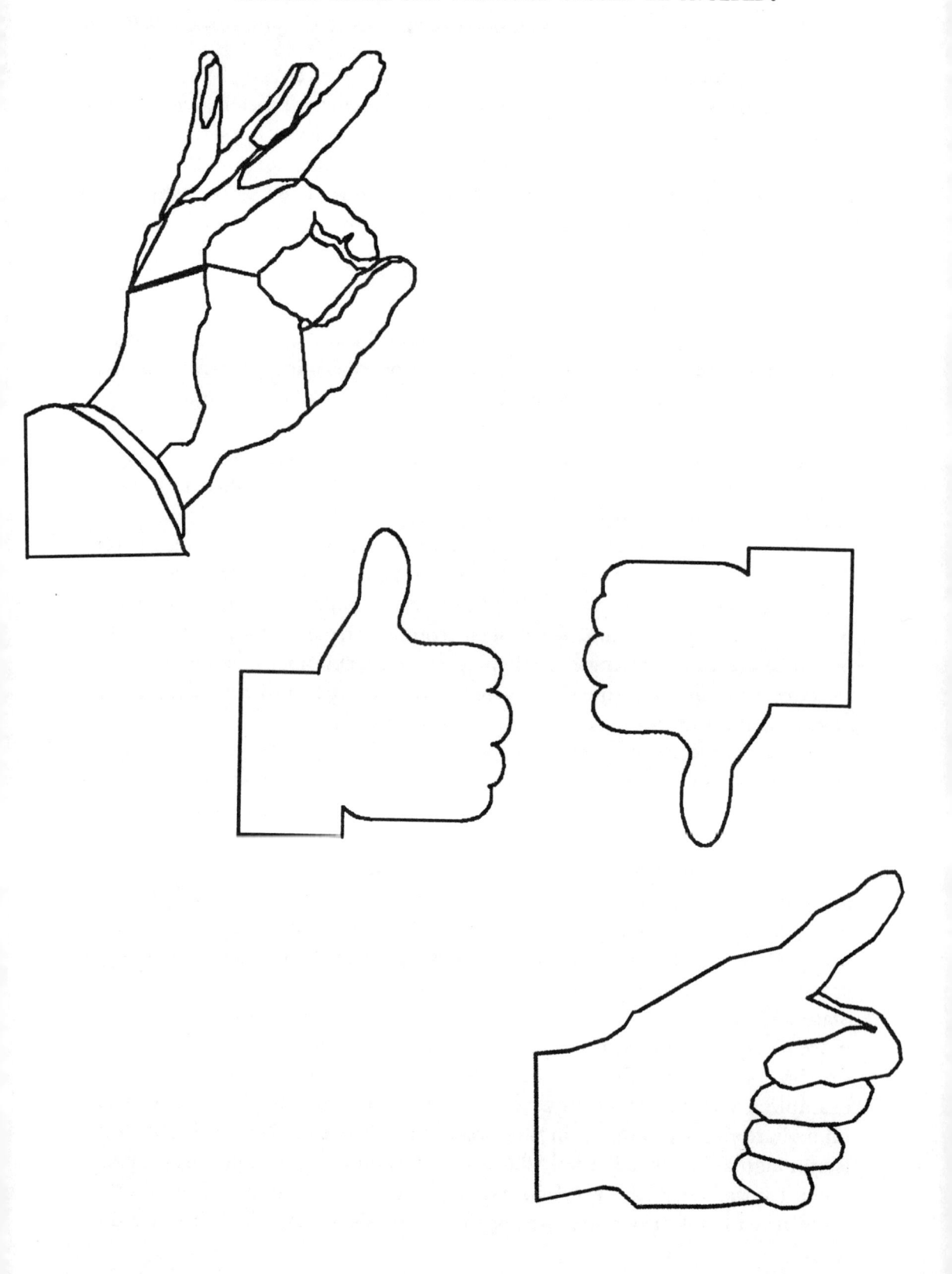

Figure 6-1

Apparently, the land available at all times, and especially during the earlier years in the United States, has created a unique American concept of space. Even now, the United States is sparsely populated. By comparison, China has five times more people on a land that is comparable in size, but of which only a fraction is inhabitable. There are so many people in China, that one barely has enough room to eat in a restaurant. As a consequence, the notion of space is differently understood than in the United States.

There are generally three kinds of space in the American interpersonal relations: INTIMATE, SOCIAL, and BUSINESS.

Typical Americans consider it an invasion of privacy or an act of aggression if someone "enters" his "breathing" space, getting close to his body. Only family members and loved ones are accepted relaxedly in this intimate space.

Social space implies a certain "elbow" distance. This is the typical distance acceptable for friends and for parties and social gatherings. Many times at international gatherings, Americans feel uneasy when a Middle Easterner, for example, intrudes into this social space. Americans perceive as aggressive, rude, or at least impolite, what others may consider a gesture of friendship and acceptance.

The Americans also distinguish a third interpersonal space of about three or four feet ideal for business or professional interaction. When people have to meet to discuss some professional matters, Americans prefer to keep their "business" distance. Many Americans are amazed, even shocked, and cannot perform normally when they meet people of other cultures who mix up the three categories.

Various studies have pointed out that Americans also tend to accept women more readily than men within their close space. This tendency could be another source of misunderstanding, because other cultures keep women at a greater distance.

The American use of space communicates to a foreigner the American history, cultural perception, and personality. Judging by the way Americans wait to get into a bus or an elevator, by how they take their seats in a bus or movie theatre, or how they stand quietly at a certain distance in an elevator, they seem to be both disciplined and respectful of others, as well as uncertain and somehow insecure in close proximity of strangers. They must also be influenced by the superior American technology and trust their systems, otherwise, they would not wait for the next bus, elevator, or train, which in many developing countries may never come.

Architecture also communicates culture and politics. American architecture is, relatively speaking, simple but functional. Nevertheless, it relays the message of freedom, experimentation, and variety. Most Americans may not be aware, however, that there is an artificial preoccupation with establishing records. Somehow, something unique must be found with every new bridge or building. By contrast, the Russians have a national obsession with grandiosity. Everything must be "bolshoy," and if something new is the biggest in the world, it makes the Russians tick, regardless of how ugly or useless it can be.

Communist architecture also reveals the crushing power of the Party. The uniformity and ugliness of the new residential quarters built in every Communist country reflect the ruling power and the nothingness to which the average citizens have been reduced. Non-Russians who have visited the Soviet Union recently also complain of a feeling of suppression caused by the new and gruesome constructions and the huge political signs found in their native lands.

Most Europeans prefer to fence in their homes and gardens. Some German homes look like bunkers. Eastern Europeans plant an almost chaotic flower garden in front of their homes. The English people prefer a green lawn. There are few fences in America and Russia, but they connote two different things: openness in the United States; collective property and, therefore, disinterest in the Soviet Union. All these strike us differently and can tell a great deal to a trained observer.

Our clothes and the way we dress for various occasions is also very telling. Clothing ourselves was, and still is, chiefly an environmental necessity, but it has become an important component of any culture. The popular costumes of any society reflect adaptation to a particular place, functionality, and beauty. The modern world has adopted the British business suit, but it has also adopted a lot of clothing items from many other cultures. One of them, and one highly prized, is the American blue jeans. A ten-gallon Texas hat may be out of place in Indonesia, but the jeans will be right at home there as anywhere else.

Clothes can show respect or disrespect, high or low status, ostentation or modesty, and acceptance or rejection of outside influences. While revealing clothes are socially acceptable in the West, wearing such clothes will be considered insulting and could entail dangerous consequences in the Middle East.

Elegant and even regular clothes are expensive in most of the world. Generally, people have few outfits, but when they dress for an occasion they can impress the Americans. There are plenty of clothes in the United States, but most visitors are awestruck by the casual to poor appearance of many people. It must be a problem of attitude. Dressing well is a show of status in the developing world, and only one of occasion in the United States. Internationally, the Americans are not reputed for elegance, except for the rich and famous; therefore, they must be reminded of the dress code for various functions. But when invited, they show up on time, in general, because punctuality is part of the American culture.

Punctuality or lack of it, or our orientation in time, is also culturally determined. For some primitive societies, even the past and the future could be mixed with the present. The notion of time differs greatly between agricultural and industrial societies and between Western and non-Western countries. Waiting for 15 to 20 minutes is considered acceptable in the West; showing up later than that is impolite or rude. Time is perceived differently in a developing and more traditional country. An American Army officer, for example, who lectured frequently in South America, concluded that even military personnel show up late there. And he said, jokingly, that they are punctual only when they plan or execute a coup. The result in everyday life can be frustrating or amusing, and people must specify whether they mean local or "American" time. Some Americans were surprised to see that their invited guests arrived two hours late. On a few occasions, some Americans were shocked when they arrived for dinner and found that the host was still in bed.

The variety of food in the world is equally matched by a variety of sitting, eating, and dining habits and manners. Without proper briefing, one can make big mistakes around a table. What we eat and drink is only partly culturally conditioned, because, after all, food must be edible, nutritious, and tasty. However, how we eat – our behavior at dinner – is completely a matter of culture.

Only patience, common sense, openness, and effort will eventually bring about the "right" behavior and relay what we want to communicate. After mastering all of these "little" things, then we can get down to serious business and can start to talk. And most likely, after we show that we know a little of the language of the other party, we will be speaking English, because English is the most common international language of the contemporary world.

ENDNOTES

1. Carley H. Dodd, *Perspectives on Cross-Cultural Communication* (Dubuque, Iowa: Kendal/Hunt Publishing Co., 1977), pp. 54-55.
2. *US News and World Report*, 18 February 1985, pp. 49-59.
3. Robert McCrum, *The Story of English* (Dubuque, Iowa: Kendall/Hunt Publishing Co., 1986).
4. Larry A. Samovar and Richard E. Porter, eds., *Intercultural Communications: A Reader*, 2d ed. (Belmond, CA: Wadsworth Publishing Co., 1976), p. 146.
5. Robbins Burling, *Man's Many Voices* (New York: Holt, Rinehart and Winston, 1970), p. 78.
6. Harry Hoijer, "The Sapir-Whorf Hypothesis," in Samovar and Porter, *Op. Cit.*, p. 153.
7. For some of the terms and translations I am indebted to my colleagues in the Foreign Area Officer Department, US Army John F. Kennedy Special Warfare Center and School.
8. See among others: *Do's and Taboos around the World*, Compiled by the Parker Pen Company (Emsford, NY: The Benjamin Company, 1985), especially pp. 37-47, and Dodd, *op. cit.*, pp. 53-59.

CHAPTER 7
ENGLISH AS AN INTERNATIONAL LANGUAGE

Introduction

English is the native language of 12 nations or some 350 million people. In addition, it is the official or semiofficial language in 33 other countries, and it is spoken to a certain degree by about 750 million people. There are more native Han Chinese or Hindi speakers, but English is by far the most international language, and it is increasingly studied throughout the world. To a native speaker, English may not pose many problems, but it does create problems for foreigners and implicitly for natives when acting internationally or cross culturally.[1]

Deceivingly Romance-root looking in its vocabulary, English is in fact of Germanic origin. To complicate matters, English has borrowed so easily from most other languages in the world, that it has actually become an open-ended language. To an immigrant like myself, English is a linguistic miracle – easy, difficult, and strange all at the same time. Above all, English is like a mountain – you could climb it for a lifetime and never reach the summit.

Soon after my arrival in the United States, I learned that the vocabulary of a preschool American child is 80-percent Germanic origin, but by the time he graduates college, his vocabulary is 80-percent Latin origin. With a good knowledge of German, French, and Latin, I tried to approach English through them, but it did not work. Obviously, English is more than the simple sum total of its parts. As the American nation is unique in the world, American English appears to be unique also. I even concluded, half jokingly, that if I had known how difficult English was, I might never have come to the United States. While doing my graduate studies I wondered which was more difficult, finishing my doctoral dissertation or perfecting my English? I defended my dissertation many years ago, but am still working on my English. To my satisfaction, however, I later realized that even native Americans must work hard if they want to skillfully master their own mother tongue.

Foreigners who learn English come across several big obstacles of which most natives are not even aware. The first is pronunciation. In fact, a foreigner must learn two English languages – the spoken one, and the written one. Most Indo-European languages have precise rules of pronunciation, but English appears to have none. "Soundly" speaking there is no difference between a tale and a tail. While "night" and "knight" are pronounced the same way, the group "ough" is pronounced in five different ways, as in tough, bough, cough, dough, and through.[2] How is a foreigner going to know the right way to pronounce them? From my personal experience, the only safe way is to ask a native, and even then it can be tricky with regard to proper names. I often wonder how future civilizations will pronounce them when they come across an English text in 10,000 years.

Then, there is the lexicon. The same word can have several meanings or can be expressed in various ways. "To get" is being used frequently in English in order to get things done, but getting its multiple nuances is not easy for foreigners. Double words and especially double-word verbs, as well as triple words such as the "little girl's room," can be puzzling to non-native speakers. Syntax, or the arrangement of various clauses in a phrase can also cause problems even when foreigners know the vocabulary. And, of course, the most difficult is the use of idiomatic expressions and jargon that are so prevalent in American English. The use of humor, figures of speech, and metaphoric language remain outside the reach of most foreigners who did not learn English from an early age. A foreigner may go through hell to learn correct English, but an American must penetrate the mind of a foreigner in order to understand his thinking and his English, which may amount to a hell as well.

"Do's and Taboos," compiled in 1985 by the Parker Pen Company, devoted a chapter to the use of English globally, explaining why "a German understands a Japanese speaking English, but neither may understand an American." Actually, following my lectures at the John F. Kennedy Special Warfare Center and School, I was approached several times by Allied students who said that they understood my language better than they understood some of the native speakers. As a matter of fact, my language, as well as the English of any foreign speaker who learned it as an adult, is less imaginative or flowery, but more simple and factual. In a way, forced by circumstances, I did what the Parker Pen Company recommends to all speakers: Keep away from complicated English. From an American standpoint, the book mentions seven causes of international misunderstanding: local color, jargon, slang, officialese, humor, vocabulary, and grammar. They raise different questions for different languages, but they all create problems of translation.[3]

Translation and Confusion

Most English-speaking foreigners use a limited number of words and tend to stick with their annotative meaning. If a word or expression has more than one meaning, as is often the case, foreigners prefer to use it in a simple, nonfigurative way. A "total disaster," for example, may mean little in a certain American context, but literally taken, it will be translated as a real catastrophe.

An American Army officer witnessed a real disaster caused recently in Malawi by the misuse of a simple word. Shortly after his arrival to the country, a young American teacher (a volunteer in the peace corps), advised his students to go on strike to protest the poor food they were served and the general poor school conditions. The students took his advice and went on strike, but "strike" in their culture implied violence and rampage. In the end, people were violent, one building was damaged, and one person lost his life. When using such words or expressions, native Americans should always remember the initial meaning of the words rather than their connotative meanings. Otherwise, it may lead to confusion and occasionally to grave consequences.[4]

Double verbs are particularly difficult to grasp, and even immigrants who spend many years in the United States can be "driven up" a wall with their meanings. "To carry on, to write off, to call in or on, to water down, or to beef up" could break somebody down. But, one can also break in, and things can break up and out in hundreds of ways only to give a lot of headaches to both foreigners and Americans trying to make themselves understood. The result is frustration and occasionally humorous. "Can you help me out?" "Sure. Which way did you come in?"

In the European languages there are also many words that look similar and actually come from the same root, but which have acquired completely different meanings. The French "demander" does not equal to "to demand" with its imperative meaning, but rather "to ask." "Patron" means owner. The Spanish "embarazado" does not mean "embarrassed," but "pregnant." If somebody translates "unadjusted" in French as "malajuste," he should know that the meaning of this word in French is actually "misfit." When written and uttered, the same words may look and sound as if they come from different worlds. "Immense" is spelled "inmenso" in Spanish, and "responsible" is . . . irresponsibly written with an a, "responsable," in French. And the American pronunciation of the Latin expression "Casus Beli" will most certainly cause the Romans to start a new war.

Even some of the most basic grammar elements do not translate easily. There is no correspondence between English and German genders, although both languages come from the same root. There is no direct equivalence for the German "der," "die," and "das." There is generally something vague, imprecise, and seemingly illogical about the gender. In my native Romanian, grammatically speaking, the dog is masculine and the cat is feminine. For years I used to refer to them as "he" and "she," although the language does distinguish between sexes. Even between two close Romance-root languages, the same nouns have irrationally acquired different genders. "Water," a basic ingredient of life, is feminine in Italian and masculine in Spanish, although the sound is similar. Moreover, within the same language, genders appear to be arbitrary. For example, in Romanian, "eye" is masculine, "ear" is feminine, "nose" is neuter, and "head" is neuter as a part of the body but masculine as a head of state.

Translating verb tenses is even more tedious, especially when two languages express differently their actions. From this point of view, English is simple by comparison with French, German, or Russian. Nevertheless, the translation must be contextual, and it is left into the hands of the interpreter or the translator.

The Italian word for translator is "tradutore," and the Italians have a saying: "Tradutore-Traditore," or translator-traitor. The "treason" is not necessarily committed on purpose, although occasionally the translator might stretch the meaning to please the audience. But it is committed because the meanings in the cultures of the two languages involved are different. Nowhere else is this more obvious than in the use of expressions and metaphors.

Certain expressions might still have some annotative meaning and could be somehow understood. "To burn a copy," for example, could have some links with a copying machine. "To pull the carpet from under someone's feet" also has some equivalent in the natural world. But could anybody translate without explaining such expressions as "to pull someone's leg," "to rain cats and dogs," "flat as a pancake," "to have a ball," and many others? How should "home run" or "foul ball" be translated in the Ukraine or any other country where baseball is not known? In an election year, Americans also "run" for office and could "deliver" a state, but if "run" and "deliver" are literally translated, the meaning is funny.

Other literary translations can also be confusing and even misleading. There is a Romanian saying that in word-by-word translation would look like getting under somebody's skin. Its meaning, however, is completely opposite to the American meaning. The German equivalent of "I am warm" is "ich bin warm," but unlike its English annotative meaning, in German the expression has sexual connotations. "Time is money" in the United States, and everybody is in a hurry. This is probably why the clock "runs" in English . . . to catch up with the people. The same clock only "walks" in Spanish translation . . . and everybody takes it easy.

Political, philosophical, and religious translations are even more difficult, because one does not simply translate such words or expressions as "Parliamentary democracy," "Lebensraum," or "the Second Coming and Last Judgment," but must explain the concept behind them. In these particular cases, seeing the tip of the iceberg or the visible/audible language amounts to nothing without knowing the ice mass or the culture beneath the surface. Inappropriate usage of such vocabulary can only create confusion while leaving a superficial impression of understanding and communication. From this point of view, the closer two cultures are, the closer the concepts behind their words, and the easier the translation of their languages. Conversely, if cultures are distant and their abstract concepts far apart, knowing the languages is not enough for a good translation.

If languages represent the greatest invention of early man, writing and printing them may be the most important innovations of modern man. However, the visual representation of a language is a further codification typical for a given language. English poses exceptionally difficult spelling problems by comparison with most European languages. While in a hotel in New Delhi, I received a message from Mrs. KRHOCEL about a meeting which had been postponed by an hour. In spite of all my efforts, I could not figure out who this person was. Later, I managed to solve the enigma when, at a party, Mrs. RHODES asked me if I received her message on time.

There are almost as many rules of writing as there are languages. German capitalizes all the nouns. Spanish uses question and exclamation marks after sentences as well as before them. And English may be the only language in which the first person singular is capitalized. Thus, "I" becomes a personality and must probably be respected as such. But English is also democratic and allows each of us to take turns and be an important "I."

Irony and humor are widespread forms of communication, but their proper use is extremely difficult. They imply a masterful use of the language and a good understanding of culture. Here are two examples: "After years of hard work and trials, the Bulgarian government gave up the idea of building a subway in Sofia. Allegedly, the authorities were afraid that the subway trains would collide with the standard of living of the population." . . . "At the fifth anniversary of his military regime, the President of Poland decided to print a stamp with his face on it. However, after checking the mail he realized that nobody was using it. He ordered an inquiry into the matter and fearing that the glue was of poor quality, he requested that only the best glue be used. Months later, still nobody was using the stamp for their mail and he summoned his prime minister to his office. 'Mr. President,' the prime minister dared to speak, 'the glue is very good, but people spit on the wrong side.'" If the point of such jokes is understood, the readers are on their way to bridging cross-cultural communication. If it is not understood, then it illustrates the difficulty of translating humor, and this is the point.

It takes years of practice to master a language to the point of telling jokes and using humor. Officials who are assigned abroad for a limited period of time will probably never be able to tell a good American joke in a local language. Even when one masters the language, the other party may not understand the culture behind it or the attitude of the American people. In addition, irony and playing purposefully with words are not only difficult, but also can be dangerous. A single mistake, a tone of voice, or a wrong smile, could occasionally be interpreted as a misplaced political allusion or, worse, as an ethnic slur. The error works both ways, but while the United States is a melting pot and most Americans are used to hearing linguistic mistakes, many people overseas are less accustomed to hearing their languages spoken by others.

Eventually, there are a few non-natives capable of assimilating English and speaking it as natives. Most foreign speakers or immigrants to the United States will retain some linguistic impediments. A notorious case is the former Secretary of State, Henry Kissinger, who arrived in the United States at the age of 14 and never lost his German accent. Even those who apparently speak English perfectly may mispronounce proper names or may encounter pronunciation difficulties when tired or angry.

From a linguistic point of view, the mind and memory seem to work in a unique way. Thinking appears to be automatic when the notions imprinted deeply on the cortex are activated by codewords that have been used hundreds or thousands of times. In general, thinking is done in the language in which the notions have been learned, and the more a certain vocabulary has been used for a given operation, the more difficult it is to change it. Many believers, for example, continue to pray in their mother tongue even when they have changed their everyday language completely. If you have doubts about someone's mother tongue, watch the way he counts. Most likely, he will multiply in the language in which he learned the operation in his formative native years. Natural interjections, such as "ouch," do not change once they have been learned in childhood, when they were imprinted on the brain. It is even said that the British who were in doubt about a German agent concluded that he was a German from the way he instinctively reacted when he was poked with a needle on his back. Speaking English perfectly is difficult for foreigners, but using it properly is difficult, even for Americans.

Problems of Misuse and Abuse

English is probably the most dynamic language in the entire world. This dynamism and "elasticity" have allowed it to borrow freely and confidently from other tongues, and to create and re-create itself continuously. It may not be the most beautifully sounding language in the world, but it is rich and precise, and it can express and accommodate everything. Nevertheless, while writers and poets explore new frontiers and create new linguistic forms of expression which add beauty and power to the language, others misuse and abuse it.

English is confronted with several dangers. One of them is a form of Orwellian "Newspeak" used inadvertently or on purpose to mislead and create the impression of change. Such language might take a variety of forms, but the final result is the same: confusion and cross-cultural misunderstanding. All of a sudden "people" become "human resources," a simple "toothpick" is called a "wood interdental stimulator," and a plain jerk becomes an "interpersonally dysfunctioning person."

Another danger is the corruption of the meaning of words. For example, a terrorist killing was reported in the press as an "execution," while the execution of a prisoner, legally sentenced to death by a jury, was referred to as "murder." The American press also refers occasionally to KGB agents in the Soviet Union as plainclothes policemen, wrongly equating them to the Western policemen. Such perverted usages could ultimately corrupt the very values of society and would not translate and read well in any other language.[5]

Americans working abroad should speak the language of the host country, at least to an acceptable degree. Even an elementary knowledge – a few sentences, greetings and courtesy expressions – can open doors, minds, and, above all, hearts. From this point of view, a little bit of knowledge is infinitely more than nothing. It shows an attitude of openness, mutual acceptance, and respect for others, which are always appreciated even when everybody knows that the real business will be conducted in English.

Remember, however, knowing a culture without speaking the language is, allegorically speaking, like being a good mechanic without having any tools to fix a car. Knowing the language without understanding the culture is like having the best tools but lacking mechanical skills. One must combine both for the best results.

Time, experience, common sense, and repeated mistakes will slowly become the best teachers for good linguistic interaction. Here are a few tips to be used, particularly in official conversations, while working overseas.[6]

- Greet foreigners in their language.

- Learn simple and courtesy sentences and use them appropriately.

- Use clear, concise, and plain English.

- Speak slowly and repeat yourself if necessary, but remember that slow speaking can also sound patronizing.

- Learn people's names and pronounce them correctly. Everybody wants to be acknowledged as a person by his or her name.

- Learn the local etiquette, and address people respectfully according to their status.

- Avoid ambiguous or connotative expressions or words, or make sure that the other party understands them as intended.

• Avoid questions which can be answered by "yes" or "no." Others may be conditioned never to say "no."

• Use visual aids whenever possible.

• Put in simple writing what you want to communicate to the other party.

• Avoid divagations and stick to the main points.

• Put numbers you use in writing and check them in both languages.

• Take some time to adjust, and also allow the other party to adjust to the language and the pace of discussions.

BE PATIENT, LISTEN CAREFULLY, AND THINK BEFORE YOU SPEAK. This is probably the sole subject where having an accent while teaching or "when writing" is useful. It is the beginning of cross-cultural communication. And if I fail to make myself perfectly clear after spending 20 years in the United States, I succeed at least in stressing the problem.

ENDNOTES

1. *US News and World Report*, 18 February 1985, pp. 49-52.
2. *Ibid.*, p. 53.
3. *Do's and Taboos around the World*, Compiled by the Parker Pen Company (Emsford, NY: The Benjamin Company, 1985), pp. 139-159.
4. Story related personally to the author by a US Army Reserve captain who worked in Malawi.
5. See for example the editorial page of *US News and World Report*, 25 April 1988.
6. See also *Do's and Taboos Around the World*, pp. 158-159.

CHAPTER 8
POLITICAL CULTURE AND COMMUNICATION

Introduction

If man could survive, prosper, and create a culture only in social groups, then group organization was necessary from the dawn of human civilization. However, group organization is not possible without politics, which makes politics as much a part of man's evolution as his language and behavior. Ancient Greeks even said that man is a political creature, and "politicking" is his way of life. But between culture and politics there is a continuous and complex interplay. Political organization is a prerequisite to any society, and it is largely the result of its culture in general and of its political culture in particular. Consequently, in order to understand the political life of a society or modern nation-state and to improve communication between cultures, we must introduce the notion of political culture which stands between culture as a collective body and behavior as a personal expression.

Political culture has been defined as the shared political values and attitudes of a population as these values and attitudes relate to the general purposes of a specific society. It has also been defined as "the set of attitudes, beliefs, and feelings about politics current in a nation at a given time."[1] The political culture of a nation is shaped by its history and by its current social, economic, and political activity. Political culture, as part of culture itself, is subjective, and it is fully shared and accepted as normal only by the members of a given society.[2] One example may illustrate this point. In order to become president or prime minister in any Western European country, one must have been active in politics for an entire lifetime. Simply, he must be a professional politician. This is "normal." An unknown farmer, for example, could never become a president in France. Americans, however, abhor politicians and find it normal to elect any decent person they trust and they see fit for the job. However, in order to get to know the future leaders, Americans put the candidates through the long and expensive ordeal of primaries, which makes no sense whatsoever in Western Europe. Thus, the political life and behavior of any society are deeply influenced by its culture, again defined as its total historical experience. It is this total experience of a society which gives meaning to its political behavior.

Ideally, a political system should represent a natural extension of a society's culture, such as common law, mores, norms of behavior, or folkways. This would allow for smooth interaction among people, harmonious social life, and gradual adjustment to change. No society, irrespective of how big and strong, can survive without continuously learning, adapting to new conditions, and changing. If political change comes gradually, and if it is absorbed by a large number of people in their daily ways, transitions and even foreign influences will not be disruptive. If a political system is imposed from outside by an alien power, or from above by an elitist group, its chances of success are limited or nil. Such political systems, superimposed in disregard of the local political culture and incompatible with the traditions of the majority of the people, could only survive by force. At best, such political systems may stay in place as a form of limited government isolated from the population. At worst, they could lead to violence and chaos and would eventually be overthrown. The post-colonial European type of political systems inherited by many African countries, for example, were confronted with tremendous problems because they did not correspond either to the political culture of the local people or to their traditional culture. As another example, the elitist pro-Western political system imposed in Iran by the Shah's government in disregard of the traditionalist culture of the population resulted in dire consequences. The strength of a political system consists in its flexibility, its ability to adjust to change, and its wisdom to keep a good balance between cultural and political behavior. To be sure, everything changes, but the speed of changes must be appropriate.

Unfortunately, political elites often reserve the rights to interpret cultural flexibility and to speed up or slow down the pace of change. They also assume a direct and persistent role in "educating" their citizens to make them accept the direction of change. In order to mobilize the population for collective action, for instance, political elites may try insistently to foster new attitudes. Pursuing their political ends, elites may resort to a variety of measures, such as subtle persuasion, propaganda, dependency relationships, coercion, or brutal repression. All of these require various forms and measures of communication between different segments of the society, but they are not universal. Like culture itself, they are typical, expected, and accepted as "normal" only in certain societies, and they are rejected, abhorred, or disregarded in others. Knowing what is expected as "normal" in a given society can help us greatly understand the political behavior of its people.

No country is culturally homogeneous, but there is enough internal cohesion in most modern countries to make behavior similar enough to permit us certain generalizations. Even when a country is deeply split among political parties, for example, most of the time the split is still done according to its political culture, which allows it to function "normally." However, international or cross-cultural political communication remains difficult, because:

- Political cultures are different.

- Political language varies from system to system.

- Political concepts are different even when language is similar.

Consequently, good political communication cross-culturally implies an equally good knowledge of culture and especially of political culture, as well as a good grasp of political terminology and its concepts. Most people are sensitive about the politics of their governments and a political mistake or an improper attitude can put an end to communication. Contrariwise, a good understanding can bridge international dialogue, and can even help to shape and to predict political behavior. A few examples of interplay between political culture and behavior can illustrate this point and should facilitate cross-cultural communication.

Comparison of Political Cultures

It is an established fact that both international negotiations at a governmental level and direct dialogue at an individual level between Americans and Russians are never easy. International negotiations are tedious and frustrating, and cross-cultural dialogue is often confusing even when those involved speak the same language and use words deceptively similar. As we already know, meaning derives from the total culture, not from language alone. The difficulty of understanding each other resides in the difference in the cultures and is exacerbated by the political cultures of the two countries. The ascent of communism during most of this century has added an ideological dimension and a new drift between the two already different cultures.

The political dictionary of the contemporary world was derived from the social organization of modern Europe. Almost every country functions according to a "constitution," and power is divided and shared by the "legislative," "executive," and "judiciary" branches of the government. Within the Western World, made up by highly developed countries and having rather homogeneous cultures, the concepts behind social and political organizations are very similar. Consequently, these countries function according to their constitutions, irrespective of being monarchies or republics and regardless of the political party in power. Authorities, including kings, obey the limits of power established by laws, and people reflect in their political behavior the accumulated culture and experience of each country. Both political systems and the people know what to expect from each other and what to accept from each other. They both initiate and adjust to change, because "change" is the permanent state of our nature.

Political concepts, for example, developed and matured slowly, allowing people to understand them, to absorb them in their daily lives, and to adjust to them. In the process, the Western World has changed from agricultural to industrial, from rural to urban, from illiterate to highly educated, and from God-centered to man-centered or secular. By redirecting its energies, the West has reached an average standard of living reserved only for kings and nobility in the past. Consequently, cross-cultural communication between various Western countries is easy because most people share many political assumptions. Outside the Western World, however, the concepts behind the same terminology vary greatly, authorities interpret political power as they see fit, and people's assumptions are vastly different.

The United States of America is a particular case of the Western World and is, in many respects, a unique country. The American Constitution and the Bill of Rights refined the European philosophy of enlightenment and combined it with basic Christian values. Within this framework, the very Declaration of Independence spoke of the "inalienable rights of the individual," of "limited government," and, more importantly, of "government with the consent of the governed." "Liberty," "dignity," and the "pursuit of happiness" became some of the most cherished values for the majority of Americans. The young nation molded these values, grew up with them, and was shaped by them to become part of the American dream.[3] For other nations, such values remained simple ideals outside the reach of their citizens. If an American, for example, assumes inadvertently that his values are equally shared and respected in the USSR, he is wrong, and his communication in that country will be impaired.

Russian Political Culture

As former Russia, the Soviet Union is a multiethnic country, and in spite of its political homogeneity, it is made up of a multitude of cultures. It is the Russian people and the Communist ideology, however, that hold the USSR together as a country. Consequently, in order to understand Soviet political culture and Russian behavior, we must understand both Russian culture and Marxism.

For a good understanding of Russian culture and political behavior, we must again penetrate the depth of the Russian "modal" personality: the historic experience of the people and their fears, prejudices, and expectations. According to knowledgeable sources, the Russians are full of dualities and contradictions. They can have great charm and can be very friendly, but by Western expectations, they can react very differently (than Westerners) even in similar circumstances. It is said that to a high degree this is a reflection of the Russian history.

The Russians enjoyed very little freedom in their history. During their formative centuries, the ancestors of today's "Russians" were subjugated, dominated, and organized by the Vikings (or "Russ"), who treated them as slaves for a good part of the time.[4] When eventually the rulers were assimilated to give birth to a new nation, much of Russia was occupied by the Tatars for about 300 years. The cruel Tatar domination left indelible marks on the modern Russian language, dress, architecture, behavior, and probably psyche as well. "Scratch a Russian and you will find a Tatar," says an East European proverb.[5] It was during the Tatar occupation and the struggle to get rid of it that "Russia" was molded together to become what it is today. Renaissance, church reformation and religious revival, enlightenment, humanism, democracy, mass education, modernization, and other benefits of the age passed the Russians by for the most part.

During their centuries-long struggle for independence from foreign rule, the Russian rulers abused power and ruled arbitrarily, and the people obeyed without questioning; they had no choice. Only together could they win and shake off foreign domination. It appears that the abuse of power by leaders and the abject submission to rulers by the people entered into the Russian character during its crucial period of cultural formation, and have remained part of it ever since. Xenophobia, or dislike for foreigners, as a case in point, is an ever-present part of the Russian scene, and it is used as a scarecrow by rulers to keep unruly people in line. Moreover, fighting to free themselves from under the Tatar "yoke" acquired a propensity of its own and gave Russia a sense of never-ending messianic mission. First, Moscow princes had to liberate the Russians. Additionally, they gathered together in a secure state the rest of the Eastern Slavs. When this job was accomplished, the tsars took upon themselves the duty to "liberate" all Christians from under Turkish or pagan domination. Eventually, tsarist Russia acquired a new name and a new mandate to "free" the entire world from capitalist exploitation. And the poor Russians never got any respite to enjoy life and freedom. As a matter of fact, serfdom was abolished in Russia only in 1861. By not knowing freedom themselves, the Russians neither understood nor respected the traditional freedom or the plight for it of other peoples they later conquered.

Like a spring that bounces back when pressure is no longer applied, it appears that once the Russians subdued the Tatars they could no longer stop their expansion. In the process, they suffered a great deal and made others suffer a lot more. They enslaved every people they came across, allegedly to liberate them; probably, the Russians kept themselves enslaved by their own system and values. When others attacked them, they complained loudly of being victimized again. When they invaded others, it was always justified as self-defense, or whatever. No political solution was good for Saint Petersburg or Moscow unless it served Russia. Occasionally, when international circumstances compelled them to give in or to withdraw from an occupied territory, it was only because at the time they did not possess enough power. As a rule, they always came back, because once the precedent was established, it gave the Russians a "legitimate" reason to be there.

There is, to this day, a certain duplicity in the Russian character that makes them both humanitarian and cruel, soft and fierce, humble and arrogant, informal and starchy, submissive to superior force and repressive when powerful, and cautious and unpredictable. And it is this combination of contradictions that accounts for the richness of the Russian "culture," from literature to music and from science to philosophy. It also appears to be a pendulum in the Russian soul swinging between extremes – the characters of the Northmen and the Tatars, representing two incompatible trends superimposed on the Slavic peasants. It seems that the two trends are still struggling to mold together and to give birth to a more settled, more stable, more reliable, and more European Russian character.

It has been postulated that the former Tatar domination and its aftermath are reflected in the Russian character as lack of confidence and an inferiority complex. As of now, the Russians indeed have a unique combination of self-esteem and self-abasement. They have a conspiratorial nature and a high degree of secretiveness and suspicion typical of the former Tatars. They also have an "Asiatic" attitude toward time, typical of the Oriental and rural societies. The Russians also display a patience unknown in the West, which, when properly put to work, translates into persistence and determination. However, unlike most people in Europe, the Russians show a high degree of indifference toward the common good, a visible insensitivity to order and neatness, and, generally, an attitude of hand-to-mouth existence.[6] They expect nothing good from political authorities and are satisfied with little, if they are left alone. Small wonder, that their often abused neighbors like to joke that Adam and Eve must have been Russians – since only two Russians could walk around naked, would eat apples, and would believe that they lived in paradise.

The political culture of Russia changed after the Bolshevik Revolution, but the attitude of the people did not change dramatically. The new government wanted to replace centuries of historical culture by brutally enforced, sweeping political decrees and to "create a new kind of man" - the socialist "Soviet man" – but this proved to be sheer utopia. Many things changed radically, but others, the more they changed, the more they stayed the same. In particular a new political jargon and terminology was introduced, but the concepts behind them have drifted farther and farther apart from their Western counterparts.

The Soviet Union and Its "Sloganry"

As if it wasn't enough that political concepts were already different, the Communist regime of the Soviet Union sought to re-educate people by changing the language, and by introducing a new political jargon and a whole array of slogans never used before. These do not permit accurate translation. In order to serve the new regime, new terms were coined and explained to the people, although, for the most part, they were little understood. Such new political terms, in existence now for over 70 years, are "dictatorship of the proletariat," "dialectic materialism," "socialist realism," and "democratic centralism." The new rulers of Russia did not invent the wheel, but they did add a number of new spokes – so many, as a matter of fact, that the Soviet wheel no longer turns.

Lenin inherited the authoritarian society from the tsars, and in many ways, he made it more oppressive. Unlike the old regime, which only controlled public life, the Communists sought to control the private lives of its people as well. Centralization of power was to be followed by centralization of economic activities and enhanced by continuous propaganda. To the innate fear of foreign invasions, the fear of capitalism and "class enemies" was added and vigorously pursued daily through the state-controlled media.

Very shortly after the revolution, the Bolsheviks lost the elections for a new Assembly, and Lenin dissolved the Assembly.[7] Thereafter, democracy acquired a new meaning, if any meaning at all, in the Soviet Union. Like the tsars before, Lenin's party began to use discretionary power. The rights of the individual or the consent of the governed were rejected by the comrades. In addition, and unlike its tsarist predecessors, the Communists also suppressed religion, previously defined by Marx as opium for the masses.

When Stalin took over, communism was well in place in the Soviet Union, and he only had to build upon the foundation laid by Lenin. The result is well known – the biggest graveyard of the world, and suffering and anguish beyond description. If Lenin would have "built socialism" (to use another slogan) the same way, is a rhetorical question now. There are no "ifs" in history. There is only one Soviet Union in the world, and Lenin, Stalin, Brezhnev, and the like, are all part of it.

Communism worked for a while in the Soviet Union because submission was part of the Russian political culture. Exhausted by World War I, many of the people supported it at first, and those who opposed it were brutally suppressed. It worked because the leaders were cunning and cruel and played their political cards well. Lenin, for instance, redirected the traditional Russian xenophobia against the "capitalist encroachment" of the young Soviet state. Then, Stalin gave new focus and purpose to the traditional Russian fear of foreigners. This time the enemy was the "Anglo-American imperialists," and the goal was the communization of the world. The Soviet people were kept in an incredible state of tension. Every day they were reminded to "safeguard the great achievements of the Bolshevik Revolution," and of the danger they endured during the Second World War. Everything had to be sacrificed to bring about the new millennium of happiness promised by Marx, which, in reality, proved more elusive than a mirage. And of course, by doing all this, the leaders managed to stay in power, to keep the Russian people busy, and to keep the other nationalities in line.

Communism survived in the Soviet Union, because it had the support of the Russian people as the dominant ethnic group in the country. The sheer size of the Soviet Union makes the Russians tick and probably compensates for their insecurity and inferiority complex. Ask a Russian if he prefers to live in freedom and prosperity in a smaller country, such as "ethnic Russia," or if he wants to police the entire USSR and continue his gloomy life. Overwhelmingly, most Russians would opt for the "bolshoy" empire, probably not even realizing that by enslaving others, they also keep themselves enslaved. The concept of "freedom," or the recent concept of "human rights," has different dimensions for the Russians.

"Human rights" are increasingly part of the current international parlance, particularly in discussions with Eastern bloc countries. Unlike the West, the Soviets have their own understanding and definition of the concept. Human rights are not defined as political rights, but as social and economic, and primarily as collective rather than individual rights. The Soviets stress, for example, the right to a job, but this carries with it the obligation to perform work. There may be a job for everyone somewhere in the Soviet Union, but it could be 5,000 miles away in Siberia, with lodging in collective quarters, and far from the family. Joblessness is not tolerated by the regimented society, and the Penal Code still provides prison terms for "social parasites" – those who do not have a job for more than three months. There is also the right to free medical care, but the system is a sham – you have to provide your own novocaine if you want to have a tooth pulled. The most recent version of the Soviet Constitution also mentions the right to housing, but it means different things to different citizens. Everyone is equal in the Soviet Union, but some people are more equal than others, to paraphrase Orwell. There are a few people who enjoy huge apartments and dachas; however, most people live in crowded quarters with many of them sharing kitchens and baths, and there is a long waiting list for those who still have nothing decent.[8]

By comparison with what they used to have, many Soviets saw their standards of living as improving for many years and somehow they accepted the system. Two things have changed this perception recently. First, the economic performance of the Soviet Union took a nosedive during the last years of the Brezhnev era, and standards of living declined visibly. Second, the younger generation of Soviet citizens are better educated, better informed, more cynical, and more individualistic. Many members of this generation have been alienated from the system and would like to change it. Can the government of Gorbachev bring about this change?

After several years in power, Gorbachev has not managed to change Soviet society much. An American who visited the Soviet Union in April 1988 described Moscow and Leningrad streets as full of potholes, dirty, and flooded because of neglect and inadequate drainage. It fits well with a recent Soviet joke which made the round in Moscow and found its way to the West. One man was digging holes on a sidewalk of a street in Moscow, followed by another man who was filling them with dirt. An old pensioner saw them and exclaimed in revolt, "Comrades, the government is paying you to work, and instead you waste our money! What are you doing here?" And one of the two men stopped and answered, "Comrade, we usually work in a team of three. I dig a hole, Ivan, who is sick today, plants a tree, and my friend here fills the hole with dirt. If Ivan is sick today, does it mean that we should stop working?"

In the fall of 1989 I took a one-month trip to the Soviet Union and saw for myself the first communist country in the world and its people. The trip took me throughout most of the European USSR, and I had the opportunity to talk to many people of various nationalities. I was deeply surprised in two contradictory ways: on the one hand, the country was still alive after decades of abuses; yet, it was obvious that Soviet society did not work any more. A Kiev cab had its windshield cracked in so many places that I felt compelled to ask the driver why he had not bought a new one. Smilingly, he answered: officially, a new windshield is 100 rubles, but in order to get it you have to pay one thousand rubles. An average salary is about 200 rubles per month. In a Kishinev restaurant, an acquaintance sneaked me through the waiting line at the door and then managed to sit me at a table with three strangers. When I left, the doorman had locked the entrance and would not let me leave without giving him two rubles. He had trouble with the other customers, he explained, and laughingly I gave him his tip. What shocked me the most, however, was the revolutionary state of mind of most people whom I met from Moscow to Kiev, and from Kishinev to Riga and Leningrad. All Soviet people want to change. They want a better life and they want it now.

Successful change in the Soviet Union implies a radical overhaul of the political system and a transformation of the Russian national character, but neither can be fixed quickly. For its entire existence, for instance, the Communist leaders kept speaking of creating a new man. As of February 1988, they still emphasize the ideal Soviet man, and they insist on defining and imposing it from above.

"This ideal man is a fighter for everything new and progressive, impassioned champion of social justice, patriot and internationalist, genuine collectivist, . . . a man with a keen sense of civic responsibility, a proper comrade, honest, decent and benevolent . . . a personality who is spiritually and physically strong and prepared to participate in the competition of minds and talents, a personality free from the mentality of consumerism and philistinism. Not a technocrat but a highly cultured person with broad horizons. Not an appendage of today's mighty technology but its master. And of course, not a 'little man' but a powerful master of life."[9]

God incarnate, one might say. What Buddha, Jesus, and Muhammad did not succeed in doing in thousands of years appears to be attainable very shortly even to the new and more realistic Soviet leaders. No wonder that when asked about *perestroika* (restructure), a young Soviet citizen answered cynically that the leaders should "*perestroika*" themselves.

Besides the conceptual differences between Americans and Russians and between capitalism and communism, there are also immense differences between institutions and organizations which otherwise seem to be similar. The Soviet Constitution, which has recently been changed, is a beautiful document and it provides for similar functions. America has a legislative branch, the Congress; the Soviet Union has a legislative branch now also called Congress. We have a Department of Interior; they also have one. But theirs is charged with maintaining domestic order, and among its many divisions is one called the KGB. The KGB might be wrongly likened to the CIA, and its new headquarters outside Moscow indeed looks like the CIA – except that the KGB equals the CIA; plus the FBI; plus the police; plus the National Guard; plus the customs services; plus prisons, labor camps, and psychiatric institutions; plus passports and visas; plus the Mafia; plus peace movements abroad; plus many other things, and minus many things as well, among which is human rights. Once all of these little details are understood, political communication between Americans and Russians is easy.

As international negotiations demonstrate, cross-cultural communication between different political systems is never easy. The difficulty of dialogue with the Soviet Union is far from being unique. Terrorist organizations "communicate" with us with bombs and explosives. We made Qaddafi eventually "understand" us only after raiding Libya. Moslem fundamentalists have a political culture of their own. The Middle East is a political powder keg. Eastern Europe is restive. It appears that political problems never stop, but this has been the condition of man ever since his beginning. The chief difference is that on the one hand, a grave political mistake today can have catastrophic consequences, but on the other hand, we now have a much better understanding of ourselves, and we also have more hopes for a better tomorrow.

Remarks

Assuming that cross-cultural communication in political discussions refers to daily contacts between average persons, here are some tips about what one should do and should understand in order to enhance political communication and to avoid grave errors.

• Read a recent political history of the host country.

• Try to understand the complex relationship between its traditional culture and its recent politics.

• Find out if the political systems stem from its own culture, or is imposed from outside.

• Find out if the average citizen genuinely participates in politics, or is indifferent, isolated, or ignored by the rulers and elites.

• Be aware that not everybody is "equal" in politics and, thus, identify them accordingly.

• Be especially aware of political sensitivities and avoid violating them.

• Avoid taking sides in host politics, unless you really know what you are doing.

• Be prepared to genuinely defend US politics when necessary and appropriate.

• As in everything else, learn from small mistakes and remember the Roman adage, "Errare humanum est; Perseverare diabolicum."

ENDNOTES

1. Gabriel A. Almond and G. Bingham Powell, Jr., *Comparative Politics*, 2d ed. (Boston: Little, Brown and Company, 1978), p. 25.
2. For a good discussion see also Samuel H. Barnes, "Politics and Culture," prepared for the Bureau of Intelligence and Research, U.S. Department of State, Political Analysis: Cultural Dimensions, Contract No. 1724-520100, 16 June 1986.
3. See among others Richard Schifter, "The Reality about Human Rights in the USSR," U.S. Department of State, Bureau of Public Affairs, Current Policy No. 920 (March 1987).
4. Robert Paul Jordan, "When the Vikings Sailed East," *National Geographic*, March 1985.
5. Vice Admiral Leslie C. Stevens, "The Russian People," *The Atlantic Monthly*, May 1952.

6. *Ibid.*
7. Richard Shifter, *Op. Cit.*
8. Michael Voslesensky, Nomenklatura (New York: Doubleday and Company, Inc., 1984); M. Wesley Shoemaker, *The Soviet Union and Eastern Europe* (Washington, DC: Sky Corporation, Stryker-Post Publications, 1985).
9. Ye. K. Ligachev, "Report on Education," CPSU Central Committee Plenum, published in *Pravda*, 18 February 1988.

Chapter 9
The World's Religions

Any soldier operating on foreign soil knows that the name of the game is communication. Particularly the soldier that is involved in Special Operations must be able to understand the worldview of a target population in order to successfully communicate and motivate. The Special Operations soldier needs to see himself as a communicator and at the same time, to understand the role of religion in cross-cultural communication.

Dr. Lloyd Kwast has developed a very useful model of culture. His approach is to see a culture as a series of levels emanating out of a core worldview.

Any communication of significance will involve all four layers of culture. The most important layer for us to focus on is worldview. We are interested in responses in the areas of behavior, values, and beliefs, but worldview is the key element in communicating.

In utilizing this model we see that religion may impact upon every level of culture. It is imperative that an area study as well as the on-the-ground operator appreciate the role of religion and its impact and daily influence on a target population. To understand another culture one must enter as much as possible into the very life and viewpoint of the native people. This viewpoint manifests itself in religious expression which embodies behavior, values, and beliefs. (See figure 9-1).

All language has its ambiguities. Religious language at times may seem ambiguous by design.

If we recall how difficult intra-cultural communication is, and the differences within a culture, we are overwhelmed by cross-cultural communication. Cross-cultural communication involves at least two processes; (1) decoding the message from one's own culture and language, and (2) encoding the message in the respondent culture (contextualizing). Contextualizing is the process by which those of a different cultures make their message understood.

Worldview as a Key to Cross-Cultural Communication

Worldview is the way people see reality. Specifically it is the way we see ourselves in relation to others. It bears emphasizing again that worldview is the best slanting point for understanding a foreign culture and religion. It is therefore beneficial for us to investigate some of the more prevalent worldviews and examples of their religious expression.

Process | **Data** | **Goal**

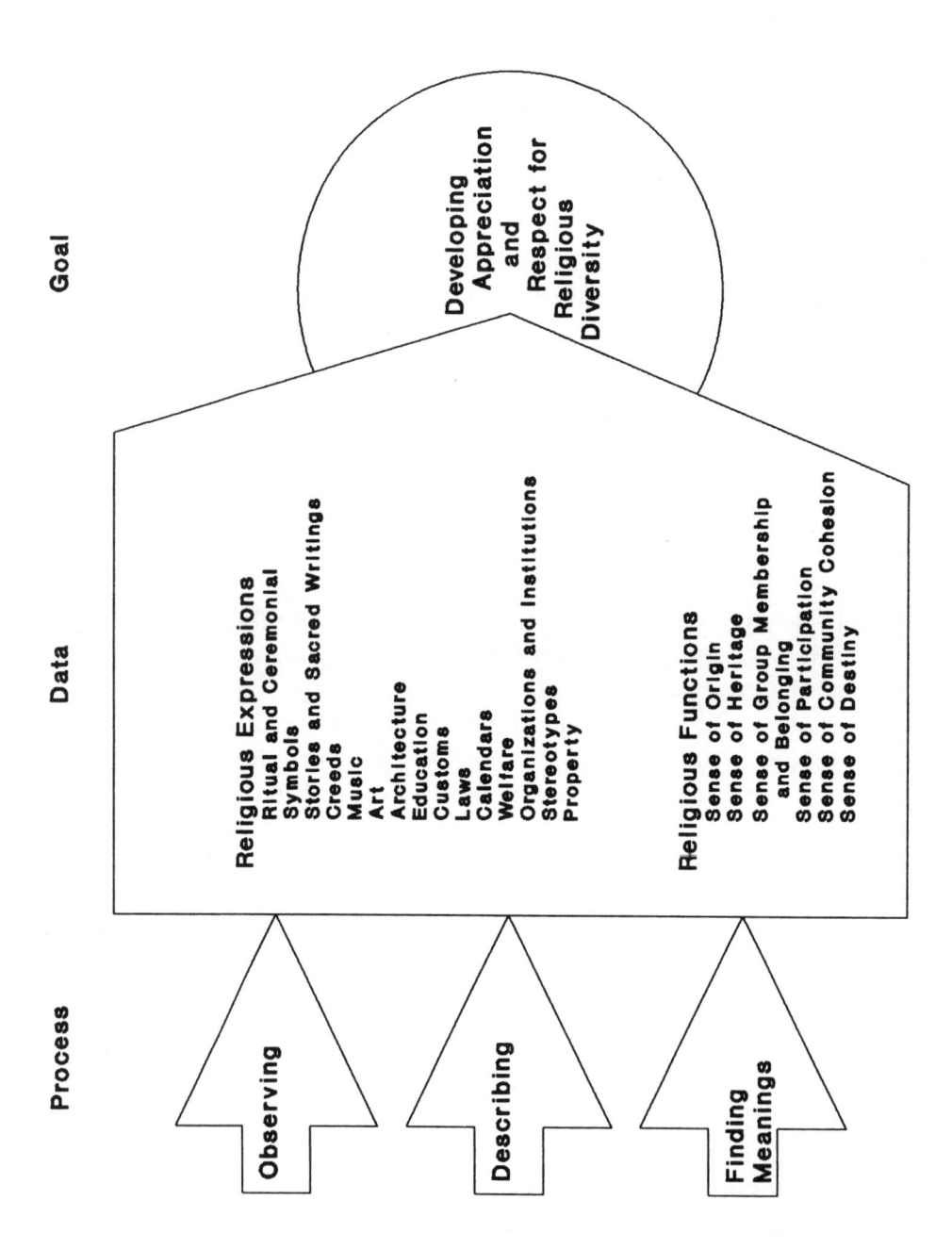

Goal: Developing Appreciation and Respect for Religious Diversity

Data:

Religious Expressions
- Ritual and Ceremonial
- Symbols
- Stories and Sacred Writings
- Creeds
- Music
- Art
- Architecture
- Education
- Customs
- Laws
- Calendars
- Welfare
- Organizations and Institutions
- Stereotypes
- Property

Religious Functions
- Sense of Origin
- Sense of Heritage
- Sense of Group Membership and Belonging
- Sense of Participation
- Sense of Community Cohesion
- Sense of Destiny

Process:
- Observing
- Describing
- Finding Meanings

Figure 9-1

The Naturalist Worldview

In the naturalist worldview the supernatural is dismissed as unimportant. Nature is very important for it is the arena in which the naturalists focus their attention. The naturalist worldview is largely a Western phenomenon. Nature may be seen as hospitable or hostile. Man is seen as a product of evolution or chance. Man's development and motivation is a product of animal instincts and drives. Time in the naturalist worldview is limitless. For many naturalists, science is god and the scientific method is their religion. Many nations which are products of communist revolutions and take-overs declare an official naturalist worldview although the population may be predominantly of another worldview. It is therefore important in the Special Operations arena for the operator to distinguish between ideal and reality. The ideology espoused by the elite leadership may be diametrically opposite of the ideology of the masses. The naturalist's worldview may be the official position of a state and yet the worldview of the populace is predominantly tribal or monotheistic. Modern examples of this phenomenon are Russia, Poland, Lithuania, and other Eastern bloc states.

THE NATURALIST WORLDVIEW

SUPERNATURE

MAN — NATURE

? PAST ⟶ PRESENT ⟶ FUTURE ?

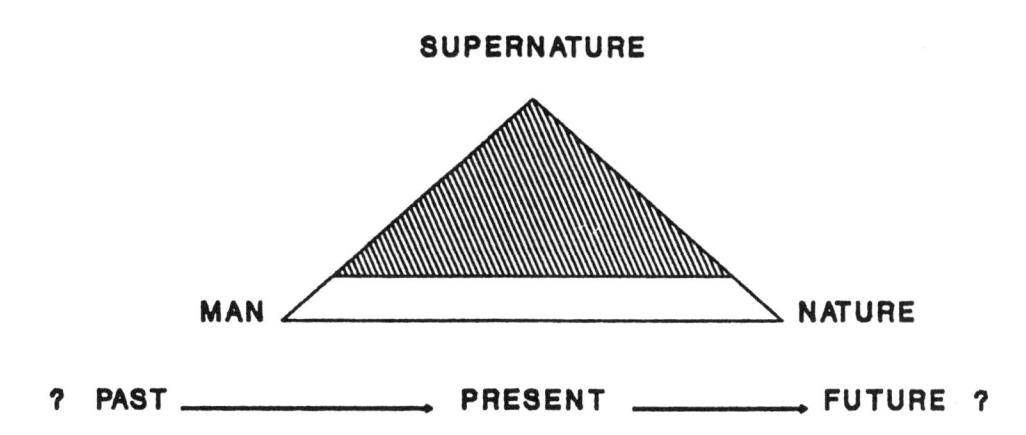

Tribal Worldview

The tribal worldview is often encountered by Special Forces Mobile Training Teams. It is focused on a plurality of gods, ghosts and spirits all interacting with the individual, family, or community. The tribal worldview is prominent in Sub-saharan Africa, Pacific islands, and with nature people groups in Asia, Australia, Siberia, and the Americas. Another term for this religious concept is "animism". As shown by the model of the tribal worldview, the natural and supernatural are intertwined and thus, inseparable. This distinguishes them from the major religions of the world.

Some of the distinction of the tribal worldview is that the individual sees himself as united with nature in such a way that he must maintain a delicate balance between all the forces for good and evil which surround him. All of nature is seen as animate. Man therefore, must guard his relationship with all the spirits within nature as well as relationships within his tribe. Often relationships with ancestral spirits must be guarded most closely. Characteristically animists utilize fetishes, charms, amulets, talismans, and special magic or medicines. Evil comes as a result of evil spirits. Secret societies and rituals are developed in order to utilize the force of evil and good spirits.

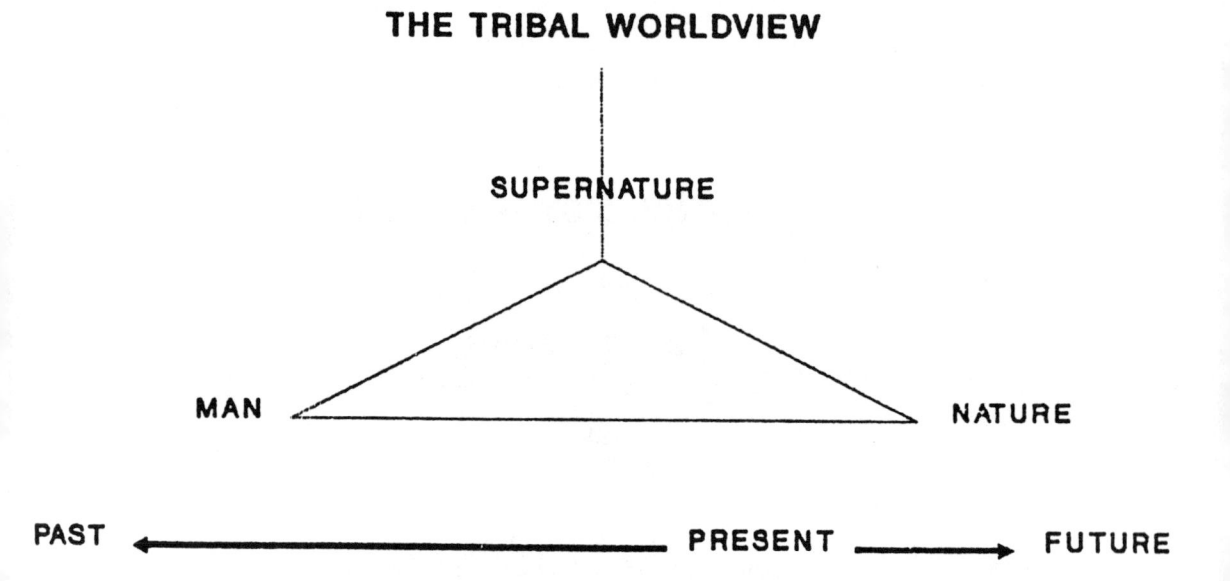

THE TRIBAL WORLDVIEW

```
              SUPERNATURE
                  /\
                 /  \
                /    \
               /      \
              /        \
       MAN  /_____\  NATURE

PAST  <------------------  PRESENT  ------>  FUTURE
```

The traditional beliefs of the Aleuts in Alaska are a classic example of the Tribal worldview. It is imperative in working with people of a tribal worldview that one appreciates the force of these beliefs and fears to bridge the communication gap.

Hindu-Buddhist Worldview

Hinduism and Buddhism developed in the same philosophical and geographical background. We may refer to this worldview as monistic or pantheistic – God as impersonal and man's focus is therefore inward. The whole universe is seen as deity.

In Hinduism, Brahman become the real, true one, the ground of all existence. A large number of deities were developed, but they were all experienced as expressions of Brahman. In this worldview, the physical world is seen as "maya" or illusion, and the spiritual world is seen as the world of reality. Linked to this are beliefs of Karma and reincarnation. The goal is to attain "moksha" or liberation from the chain of reincarnation. The caste system is an intrinsic part of the Hindu worldview.

The Buddhist worldview is similar and yet distinct from the Hindu worldview. Karma and maya are universally accepted. The goal of many is to escape this world of suffering and move into Nirvana or an existence of nothingness. Man's destiny is in his own hands. The daily attitudes and behavior of the Hindu and Buddhist people are deeply influenced by these religions and philosophies.

Chinese Worldview

The traditional Chinese worldview can not be ignored for more than one billion people are ethnically Chinese. Central to the Chinese worldview is the belief that man and nature are inseparable and interdependent. Man and nature have a common origin in the "Tao". Tao is the path the universe follows and manifests itself in the "Yin and Yang". The Yin-Yang are balanced in the five ordinate elements of fire, water, earth, wood, and metal. Though the Yin and Yang oppose one another, they are in a dualistic tension and balance. Everything in nature is either Yin or Yang. Associated with Yang are the positive elements such as heaven, light, heat, masculinity, life, etc. The Yin includes the opposite elements: earth, dark, cold, femininity, death, etc. The world around is filled with good and bad spirits which impose some control over nature. Anything which could upset these forces is to be avoided at all costs. We can see in the Chinese worldview the deep influence of a tribal worldview super-imposed on the Yin-Yang system. Lao-tze and Confucius contributed profoundly to the Chinese worldview. Confucius emphasized drawing from the wisdom of the past in relation to social relationships. Lao-tze emphasized the present and balance with nature. The elements of all of these are manifested as religion and philosophy.

Monotheistic Worldview

Judaism, Christianity and Islam share a monotheistic worldview. There is a personal God who created an orderly universe. This personal God is active in the affairs of mankind and the universe. He reveals Himself through nature and communicates with man.

The ramifications of the monotheistic worldview can be seen in the beliefs, sacred literature and practices of these three major faiths which encompass almost half of the world's population.

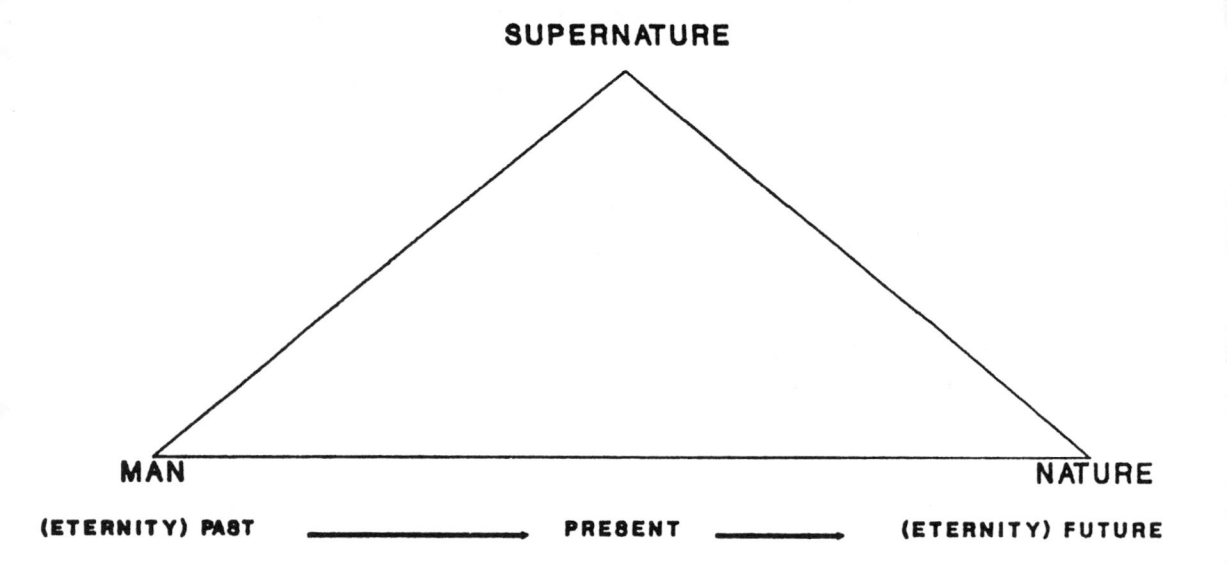

```
              SUPERNATURE
                  /\
                 /  \
                /    \
               /      \
              /        \
             /          \
            /            \
           /              \
          /                \
         /                  \
        /                    \
       /_____\
     MAN                      NATURE
(ETERNITY) PAST ————▶ PRESENT ————▶ (ETERNITY) FUTURE
```

Since no religion can be understood apart form its historic and social context, the following pages will address the background, beliefs, and effects on military service of these three important religions.

Judaism

Judaism is not only a reflection of the Hebrew community, but it must be understood through the national history of the Jews as God's chosen people. No other religion reflects this character.

The central belief is in Yahweh as the one and only God who made a covenant with Abraham and his descendants that is still valid today. God's expectations were expanded in the Ten Commandments:

1. I am the Lord your God.
2. You shall have no other gods before me.
3. You shall not take the name of the Lord your God in vain.
4. Remember the Sabbath day to keep it holy.
5. Honor your father and mother.
6. You shall not murder.
7. You shall not commit adultery.
8. You shall not steal.
9. You shall not bear false witness.
10. You shall not covet.

Worship consists of reading the Scriptures and prayers of praise and petition. The synagogue must have at least ten male Jews to conduct a worship service. Prayers are done facing Jerusalem. Daily prayers are offered in the morning, afternoon, and evening.

During the year the following days are considered holy: The Sabbath is weekly day of rest from sundown on Friday until sundown on Saturday. The Passover is a celebration of the escape from exile in Egypt. Rosh Hashana is the Jewish New Year, which comes in September or October of our calendar. Yom Kippur is ten days after the New Year and is a day of confession, repentance, and reconciliation. Hanukkah celebrates the victories of the Maccabees and cleansing of the Temple. Purim celebrates the intervention of Queen Esther during the exile in Persia. Shabouth or Pentecost occurs 50 days after Passover and is a harvest festival. Sukkoth, the Feast of Tabernacles, is also a harvest festival.

Two rituals are vivid reminders of the covenant relationship of God with the Jewish people. The first is circumcision, which takes place on the eighth day after the birth of a male child. The second is the Bar Mitzvah of the 13-year-old boy who has completed his studies and thereafter is considered an adult member of the community.

The foundations of Judaism are in the covenant relationship with Abraham and his descendants. He was a chieftain of a semi-nomadic tribe, circa 3000 B.C., in Ur of the Chaldees in Mesopotamia. He led his family to the area of modern Israel. There they established themselves and multiplied. The faith developed on the concept of one God with whom man had an interpersonal relationship. The covenant was further expanded through Moses who led the Israelites out of bondage in Egypt. He received the Ten Commandments from God on Mount Sinai. He was also the human author of the first five books of the Jewish Bible. Their Bible also includes the writings of the Prophets and other wisdom literature. In addition to the Bible, the Talmud (civil and canon law), the Gemara (rabbinic commentary on the unwritten law and oral tradition), and the Midrash (directions for daily living) are authoritative.

Orthodox Judaism attempts to adhere to the Talmudic teachings of kosher food preparation, observance of the Sabbath laws, and circumcision.

Conservative Judaism seeks to retain the essentials of the faith by following the feasts and reinterpretation of the Law in the light of modes or times while avoiding the tendencies toward assimilation found in Reform Judaism.

Reform Judaism seeks to adapt the faith to the society in which it exists. It lays aside the practices of the Talmud and changes worship from the Sabbath service to a Sunday service. The emphasis is on worshipping God and ethical living.

Islam

Islam is a religion founded by a prophet, Mohammed. He was born in the year 570 A.D. in the city of Mecca in Arabia. He began to receive revelations from God through the angel Gabriel at the age of 40. His sharing of the revelations with the people of Mecca was not well-received, and he fled with some followers to Medina. His message was well-received there and he built a new religious community based on his teaching. He then sought to unite all Arabs as brothers under the new faith. He was willing to use force and expediency to further his goals and was very successful in uniting the Arabs and eventually capturing Mecca. He died in 632 A.D., two years after capturing Mecca. There was a long period of confusion following his death, as he had not designated a caliph (successor). Many of the disputes in the Middle East throughout history, and even today, are centered on authority and the proper line of succession.

There are "Five Pillars" of Islam. The first is the creed – "There is no God but Allah, and Mohammed is the messenger of Allah." The serious recitation of this makes one a Muslim. The second is a prayer (Salah), which is recited five times a day. Friday noon prayer is the weekly public worship. A ritual washing precedes prayer. In the desert, sand is substituted for water. The third pillar is alms giving (Zakat) for the faith and for the poor. The fourth is fasting (Siyyam), which is a period of 30 days in the ninth month of the lunar calendar and forbids food, drink, smoking, sexual intercourse, and shedding blood during daylight hours. The festival of Ramadan follows the fast. The fifth pillar is the pilgrimage (Hajj). The trip to Mecca is a lifetime goal of every Muslim who is physically and financially able to make the trip. The Ka'ba, a huge building veiled in black silk, holds the Black Stone that they believe was brought from heaven by an angel. Abraham built a shrine for the Black Stone, assisted by his son, Ishmael, from whom Muslims claim descendancy.

Additional practices of Islam include circumcision, the veil (Purdah) for Muslim women, polygamy, and the avoidance of eating pork.

Islam is not only a belief system, but is a way of life, a total system that governs all aspects of a Muslim's life. Faith for muslims is a state of happiness acquired by virtue of positive actions. The Holy Qur'an and the Traditions of Mohammed establish the standards of faith. Muslims profess:

> 1. The belief in God, angels, Holy Books as completed by the Qur'an; his messengers with Mohammed being the last of them all; the Day of Final Judgement; the absolute knowledge and wisdom of God.

THE WORLD'S RELIGIONS   113

2. True believers will trust God always and enjoy unshakable confidence in Him.
3. To utilize wealth, life, health, and knowledge in a manner pleasing to God.
4. To participate in daily prayers (five times).
5. To pay religious taxes (alms or Zakah) to the rightful beneficiaries. (The minimum is 2.5 percent of annual net income.)
6. To use every means at ones disposal to combat evil.
7. To obey God and His Messenger, Mohammed, and love their fellow men.
8. To show genuine kindness to guests, particularly strangers.
9. To speak the truth and engage in good talk or remain silent.

Christianity

The name "Christian" was applied to the followers of Jesus Christ. A Christian is generally one who professes the belief that Jesus Christ is the Son of God and seeks to order his or her life in accordance with the teachings and example of Christ. Jesus Christ was born of a virgin in Palestine about 4 B.C. Christians believe He was the promised Messiah of the Old Testament. He began his public ministry at about age 30 and was crucified at about age 33. Christianity is unique in that its founder rose form the dead. Following his ascension his followers established and spread the Church. Most Christians profess the following beliefs:

1. That there is one God, but we experience Him through the three Persons (Father, Jesus Christ the Son, and the Holy Spirit).
2. That the Bible is the revealed Word of God.
3. That there will be a day of reckoning when the world will be judged and everyone will spend eternity in either heaven or hell.
4. That the angels are messengers of God, and that the devil is a fallen angel.
5. That supernatural events or miracles are used by God to confirm His word and power.

There are three major branches of Christianity: Roman Catholic, Orthodox, and Protestant.

Roman Catholics are found worldwide but are the strongest in southern and central Europe and Latin America. The Catholic faith has the following distinctive characteristics:

1. The Pope in Rome is the head of the Church and is considered infallible when speaking *ex cathedra* (from the chair) on matters of faith and morals.
2. Purgatory is a temporary, intermediate state between heaven and hell.
3. There are seven sacraments – Baptism, Eucharist, Confession, Confirmation, Marriage, Holy Orders, and Last Anointing.
4. The Bible is viewed as a gracious guide in the teaching mission of the Church and is to be interpreted by priests.
5. Worship focuses around the mass, which is the eucharist of unleavened bread and wine that becomes the body and blood of Christ.
6. The Church functions as a hierarchy of priesthood under the Pope.
7. Most Roman Catholics are Western Rite, but there are about 20 groups of Eastern Rite Catholics who hold identical beliefs and recognize the authority of the Pope, but differ in language, liturgy, customs, and tradition.

* The Orthodox Church separated from the Church of Rome about 1054 A.D. The Eastern Church used Greek in the beginning as its liturgical language. Other differences grew over the authority of the Pope, worship, traditions, and creed.

1. Orthodox believe that God is one in three persons, but believe that the Holy Spirit proceeded directly from God the Father and not from both Father and Son as Catholics believe.
2. The two main sources of Orthodox faith are Holy Scripture and Holy Tradition. The Orthodox affirm the Nicene Creed, the first seven ecumenical councils, and the writings of the church fathers. The Nicene Creed is recited at all services.
3. Orthodox believe the church is the mystical body of Christ. It is a local community of believers who gather to celebrate the Lord's Supper.
4. Salvation comes through the Church and faith in Christ's atonement. The Last Judgment will be at Christ's second coming.
5. The Orthodox also have seven sacraments, which are called mysteries: Baptism (of infants or adults by immersion), Confirmation (called Chrismation), Eucharist, Penance, Anointing of the Sick, Marriage, and Orders.
6. The policy of eastern Orthodox Churches is through the Bishops who trace their succession to the Apostles. Eastern Orthodox Churches have also been developed along national lines.

The roots of Protestantism are in the apostles of the first century as well as the foundation theology of the Catholic Church. The reformers of the fifteenth and sixteenth centuries (Hus, Luther, Zwingli, etc.) led a protest against some of the abuses of the Church during the Middle Ages. The number of protestant denominations is myriad. This study will focus on major Protestant faith groups: Baptist, Methodist, Anglican, and Lutheran.

Baptist history begins in the early 16th century in Europe with the Anabaptists, who believed that only adults rather than infants should be baptized. John Smyth, an English Separatist preacher living in Holland to avoid persecution, was impressed by Anabaptist believers. He set up the first baptist Church in Amsterdam in 1609. Due to persecution, Baptists fled to the colonies. During the Revolutionary War their numbers increased greatly due to their belief in religious liberty. Major growth also occurred in the early 19th century along with expansion on the Western frontier. Most Baptists are found in North America. Baptists are individualistic and emphasize the separation of church and state.

Methodism was founded by John Wesley, the son of an Anglican priest. The term Methodist comes form the methodical prayer and study habits. Methodism's greatest growth occurred in North American because of lay preachers (circuit riders) who spread the Word on the frontier. Methodists are tied to no particular creed, and doctrinal positions are reached in conference by free inquiry within the limits of scripture, tradition, experience, and reason.

In the 16th century many English Church and lay people were anxious for dramatic changes from the Catholic Church. When King Henry VIII wished to annul his first marriage and the Pope refused, Henry ordered the Archbishop of Canterbury to reject papal authority. The king was then recognized as the new head of the church of England. At first Catholic sacraments, creeds, and orders were kept. The reformation that was going on in mainland Europe greatly influenced the Anglican Church; the service was simplified and the Bible was translated into English. Anglicans accept two sacraments, Baptism and Holy Communion. Five additional sacramental acts are observed – Confirmation, Penance, Holy Orders, Unction, and Marriage.

The Lutheran Church began in January, 1521 as a result of the excommunication of Martin Luther, a German priest, for questioning some of the beliefs and practices of the Catholic Church. He emphasized salvation through faith rather than through the institutions of the Church. Luther's reformation was supported by many of the secular princes of Germany and Scandinavia.

Lutherans practice two sacraments: Baptism by sprinkling to infants and believing adults and Holy Communion. The sacraments are believed to be channels of God's grace. In addition, rites of the Lutheran Church are confession and absolution, confirmation of baptismal covenant, ordination of ministers, marriage, and a ministry to the sick and dying.

Conclusion

Overall, religion has an impact on the way soldiers react in a military confrontation. Islam has exuded a warlike spirit throughout its history. Islam, a religion of power, is also a missionary religion. The combination of power and missionary zeal results in a faith that seeks to dominate. Since church and state are one in Islam, there is an increasing tendency to identify nationalism with Islam and national culture with Islamic culture. Therefore, these nations are placed on a collision course with other faiths and non-Muslim nations.

The modern Muslim soldier and terrorist, whose warrior spirit is well known, may be motivated by the promise of paradise and notoriety encouraged by religious zealots. Moreover, the terrorist is strongly motivated by his image as a freedom fighter and a guarantee of martyrdom. However, a Muslim's instinctive feeling is that the practice of his religion cannot be reconciled with living under a non-Muslim government. The Muslim soldier displays a fierce determination and willingness to die for religious causes. Therefore, religious leaders, who are strong motivators for military service and zeal, are afforded opportunities to extend the power of Islam through conquests.

In the case of Judaism, Jews have resisted serving in the military in Russia and Poland from a faith perspective since they could not continue their faith and life-style, for in the past conscription was often for life.

Since the establishment of their own state, Jews are seen as being very militant. Yet, history has shown that Israel fights for nationalism, spurred on by Zionism and a survival imperative, not solely for religious beliefs. Masada, a virtually impregnable mountaintop fortress in southeast Israel, has become a symbol of Jewish nationalism. After the destruction of Jerusalem in 70 A.D., Masada was the last bastion of Jewish rule. It took a Roman army of 15,000 almost two years to conquer the zealots, who numbered less than 1,000 including women and children. While only seven women and children survived, the remainder committed mass suicide rather than surrender to the Romans. The determination of the Israeli soldier of today is that the events of the Masada will never happen again. For Jews the world over, Masada remains a symbol of freedom and resistance. Commemorative stamps and medals bear the inscription, "Masada shall not fall again." Recruits of the Israeli Defense Forces are brought there to swear on oath to that effect. Therefore, there is a firm resolve that the nation will not allow itself to be conquered by outside forces again.

Christianity reflects a wide variance in faith and practice, which is also expressed in the military service. Some Christian groups have been extremely militant while others have emphasized pacifism.

Historically, Eastern Orthodox and Roman Catholic churches have been the most militant. The church and the soldier have often moved forward as one. However, on the opposite spectrum have been the issues of conscience for Anabaptists as well as other Christian groups that have taken a position of pacifism. It would appear that if the relationship between religious devotion and specific social commitments has not been clarified effectively, the result may be the alienation of membership caused by mixing politics with religion. Therefore, the impacts these beliefs and values have on the way these soldiers fight may be in large part extrinsic to the merits or demerits of the war itself.

In speaking of religion and cross-cultural communications we are forced to use generalities which are fraught with exceptions. We must move beyond the temptation in doing cultural and area studies to simply categorize people as Christian, Muslim, etc. and not recognize that below the surface are deeply held worldviews which may seem contradictory to the Monotheism which is publicly practiced. Just as we recognize layers of culture there may be layers of indigenous faith and practice. It is also difficult for Westerners to appreciate the eclectic manner in which others in the world choose not to exclusively align themselves with a single faith or dogma. In the special operations arena it is imperative that the soldier develop a deep appreciation for indigenous religions and their deep implications for the daily life of their adherents.

ENDNOTES

Most of the information in this chapter has come from David J. Hesselgrave, *Communicating Christ Cross-Culturally* (Grand Rapids, MI: Zondervan Publishing House, 1978); J.N.D. Anderson, *The World's Religions*, (Grand Rapids, MI: Eerdman's Publishing Co., 1966); R. Pierce Beaver, et. al., eds., *The World's Christianity and Culture* (Maryknoll, NY: Orbis Books, 1981); Charles H. Kraft, *Communication Theory* (Nashville: Abingdon Press, 1983). Most graphs also come from David J. Hesselgrave's book.

Chapter 10
Concluding Remarks

General Remarks

There are thousands of languages in the contemporary world and numerous cultures and subcultures. No one can possibly completely comprehend more than a few of them. Consequently, in this manual I have tried to focus on the causes of cultural diversity rather than on individual cultures. Nevertheless, by understanding the big picture and by placing American culture in proper perspective, it is possible to develop a better approach to communication.

I strongly recommend that this manual be used with extensive audiovisual aids that illustrate cultural differences and suggest ways to bridge them. I also suggest that students and guest speakers be invited to share their experiences and knowledge in cross-cultural settings. Numerous Americans have served overseas, and their experience could be used as powerful teaching tools to be shared in the classrooms.

The manual has tried to address the most important aspects of cross-cultural communication, but many other aspects have been left out. Students should always remember that in the final analysis, each person is unique, and yet he is enculturated in a given society. As complex creatures, we might be many persons in one, but in today's world of nation-states, we should respect everyone for his individual traits as well as for the culture of the country that produced him.

Americans, for example, should be able to identify the chief US cultural traits. However, great as it may be, the American culture is only one of many. What is good, normal, and desirable in the United States will not necessarily be good, normal, or desirable somewhere else. Consequently, one must modify his behavior and his cultural expectations to meet the new challenge.

As a unique person, you can be a man or a woman (young or old), you can come from a certain social group or class, and you may enjoy a privileged status. Various cultures place different degrees of importance to any one of these particular traits. Assuming inadvertently that other cultures treat men and women equally, as one example, could actually impair the process of communication. Individuals can adjust rather easily in their daily conduct, but cultures change very slowly. Treating others both as individuals and as bearers of their cultures will enhance your chances of communication. If the culture shock, or at least some of its symptoms, is inevitable, a good preparation for an overseas assignment can soften its effects and will allow you to start to perform well shortly after your appointment.

Preassignment Preparation and First Contacts Abroad

Your cross-cultural preparation probably started long ago when you first met people coming from other cultures or when you first traveled abroad. Purposeful preparation, however, requires a new effort which changes gradually from understanding cultural generalities to learning political and economic details about a given country. Once you know the country of your assignment, you must start your specific preparation. A good geography book will help you understand the physical environment. A history book will help you know the people, and a recent political history should provide you with an understanding of that country's social organization. Then, you should focus on the culture – customs, behavior, attitudes, values, beliefs – that will surround you there in your work and daily life.

There are numerous sources of written information on virtually every country, but it is difficult to get the "feeling" of any culture only from books. Current literature and magazines from the country can help fill the gap to a high degree if you know the language, but a good session with a person from that country, if available, will be a lot better.

Before leaving for your country of assignment, there are certain practical things to be solved and done, and from this point of view existing literature can be helpful. For example, legal requirements such as visas, customs regulations, immunization certificates, and so on, vary from country to country. The State Department, other governmental agencies, as well as individual foreign embassies in Washington, should be able to answer any of your questions. Nevertheless, despite any preparation, a few problems will always be left to be confronted head-on abroad, and they may arise at the airport.

From my own experience, I found out that the first formalities after arrival – the first hours, the trip from the airport to a hotel, and the first few days in the new country – are the most difficult of all. It is during this time that money changers, drivers, porters, intermediaries of all sorts, and crooks will try to take advantage of the newcomer. The only solution to circumvent the situation is by having someone waiting for you at the airport. Otherwise, even the experienced traveler could encounter obstacles and problems.

The next step, and a very important one, is to establish a local contact who can offer you important advice and who can help you avoid violating local taboos. Religion, politics, and the role and place of family and women, for example, are delicate topics everywhere. An inappropriate attitude toward anyone of them can be considered very offending in many cultures and could greatly reduce your efficiency.

CONCLUDING REMARKS 121

Eventually, you will learn the local customs and will adjust your behavior without compromising your values and beliefs. You will also learn from making mistakes, but it is highly desirable that you avoid repeating them. While there are no lists of DO's and DON'Ts with universal value, here are some tips promoting effectiveness most everywhere, as well as suggestions for better cross-cultural communication.[2]

- TASK BEHAVIOR

Promote:	Avoid:
HARMONY	INITIATING ALL IDEAS
MEDIATION	INFORMATION EMPHASIS
COMPROMISE	IDEA EVALUATION

- PERSONAL BEHAVIOR

Promote:	Avoid:
COOPERATION	REJECTING OTHERS' IDEAS
PARTICIPATION	GROUP MANIPULATION
GROUP ORIENTATION	ASSERTING AUTHORITY

- MAKING JUDGMENTS

Promote:	Avoid:
CAREFUL LISTENING	HASTY JUDGMENTS
FEW INTERRUPTIONS	TIME PRESSURE
POSITIVE EVALUATIONS	NEGATIVE STATEMENTS

- HANDLING AMBIGUITY

Promote:	Avoid:
TOLERANCE FOR UNCERTAINTY	DISPLAYING IRRITATION
TOLERANCE FOR FRUSTRATION	HOSTILITY
ACCEPTANCE OF POWERLESSNESS	SHOWING FRUSTRATION

- DISPLAY OF RESPECT

Promote:	Avoid:
EXPRESSIONS OF RESPECT	ATTITUDE OF SUPERIORITY
CONFERRING STATUS	SELF-IMPORTANCE
ENHANCE ESTEEM OF OTHERS	DISRESPECT
ENCOURAGING WORDS	DISREGARD
ACCOMPLISHMENTS OF OTHERS	DISBELIEF

- PERSONALIZING KNOWLEDGE AND PERCEPTIONS

Promote:	Avoid:
RECOGNITION OF OWN CULTURE	STEREOTYPING OTHERS
RECOGNITION OF OTHER'S WAYS	"HARD SELL" OF OWN IDEAS

- DISPLAYING EMPATHY

Promote:	Avoid:
DISPLAY INTEREST	INSINCERITY
SEE OTHER SIDE	SUPERFICIALITY
PUT SELF IN OTHER'S SHOES	NON-CARING ATTITUDE

- TAKING TURNS

Promote:	Avoid:
SHARE RESPONSIBILITY	MONOPOLIZING TALK
SHARE DECISIONS	PATRONIZING TALK
SHARE START AND CLOSE OF DISCUSSION	NEGLECTING RECIPROCITY
	HASTE IN TIME
ELICIT IDEAS	

Suggestions for Better Human Relations and Cross-Cultural Communication[3]

REMEMBER THAT WHEREVER YOU GO THERE IS ALREADY AN AMERICAN CLICHE PRECEDING YOU.

Try to understand and discern this cliche and you may be able to slowly improve it.

ESTABLISH YOURSELF AS A PERSON.

Though you are an American, you are also a unique person, and as such you can and you should break any unwarranted ethnic stereotype.

TAKE YOUR TIME AND SLOW DOWN WHEN APPROPRIATE.

Remember that in many countries, Americans are perceived as too quick, too direct, too wordy, and always under time pressure.

GREET PEOPLE AND SPEAK TO PEOPLE.

There is no substitute for a cheerful word of greeting.

CALL PEOPLE BY THEIR NAMES.

People's names are very dear to them, and this is even more important when you work with or meet the same people again.

BE AWARE AND RESPECTFUL OF STATUS AND AGE WHEN TALKING TO PEOPLE.
They are very important in various cultures and very different than in the United States.

BE FRIENDLY AND OPEN.
Act friendly and you will be perceived as such. Conversely, you will be perceived as cool, distant, and unfriendly, irrespective of how you feel "inside."

BE CORDIAL.
Act as if everything you do is pleasant, and most people will reciprocate.

SMILE AT PEOPLE WHEN APPROPRIATE.
It does not cost anything and it can open hearts.

ESTABLISH CONTACTS.
Make friends, show interest and visit local people, and they will also open up to you.

OBSERVE AND RESPECT THE LOCAL DRESS CODE.
Remember that revealing clothes are considered offensive in many countries.

AVOID CARELESS POSTURE.
Slouching in a chair or showing the soles of your shoes is considered rude in many places.

RESPECT LOCAL FOOD AND TABLE MANNERS.
Be reasonable and understanding even if they do not fit your taste.

BE AWARE OF LOCAL TIME CONCEPTS.
It will help you avoid frustration and occasional embarrassment.

BE GENUINELY INTERESTED IN PEOPLE WITHOUT BEING PUSHY.
While others can learn from you, you can also learn from others.

BE RESPECTFUL OF WOMEN.
They are the mothers of the world.

BE ALERT OF THE PLACE OF WOMEN.
In many societies their place and treatment is very different than in the

United States.

BE VERY RESPECTFUL OF OTHER RELIGIONS.
They give mankind some of our most profound beliefs.

BE AWARE OF POLITICAL IDEOLOGIES.
In most non-democratic societies they are sensitive topics of discussion.

DO NOT UNDERESTIMATE OTHERS.
Most people are intelligent and have enough common sense to be your equal, irrespective of their formal education, social status, and wealth.

BE GENEROUS WITH PRAISE AND CAUTIOUS WITH CRITICISM.
Remember, however, that too many compliments may trigger a negative reaction. Remember also that admiring an object too much may compel a host to give it to you as a present.

BE CONSIDERATE WITH THE FEELINGS OF OTHERS.
Otherwise, you may hurt people inadvertently.

DO NOT "SHAME" ANYONE.
Saving face is extremely important in many countries, and people do not like to be embarrassed.

BE PREPARED TO EXPERIENCE THE UNKNOWN.
America is not the world and the world is not America.

STOP COMPARING EVERYTHING TO THE AMERICAN CULTURE.
The world is diverse and complex, and besides, not everything back home is perfect.

BE ALERT TO OFFER HELP AND PROVIDE SERVICES.
What we do for others is most important in life, yet others may place unreasonable demands on us which will be impossible to meet.

AVOID CONTRADICTING PEOPLE AND ALSO SAYING "NO."
A frank "No" is not acceptable in the Far East, for example. Silence, or an evasive answer will be more readily accepted.

TRY TO END ANY DISCUSSION ON A POSITIVE NOTE.
Life is a series of compromises; things that do not seem good today, may

improve in the future.

RETURN FAVORS WITHIN THE PRESCRIPTIONS OF YOUR ASSIGNMENT.
However, you must be aware of the local etiquette of gift exchanging.

BE CAUTIOUS WHEN MAKING PROMISES.
An inflexible position will not help you, but a broken promise will certainly hurt you.

STRESS FORMALITY.
At least until you become fully familiar with the place.

CULTIVATE A SENSE OF HUMOR.
But remember that humor does not translate easily and could be misinterpreted with negative consequences.

BE PREPARED TO LEAVE TIPS WHEN AND WHERE APPROPRIATE.
It is a way of life in many countries.

DO GIVE SOME SMALL CHANGE TO BEGGARS.
Begging is a sign of social "health." It means that there is enough social freedom to allow people to beg, and that some people have enough to give the extra to the needy. Remember that turning your back to the beggars may leave a bad impression with the local people, but giving everything you have to beggars could make you one of them as well.

DO KEEP A STASH OF DOLLAR BILLS IN ONE OF YOUR POCKETS.
They come in handy, and are appreciated on many small occasions.

IF WORKING IN A SENSITIVE CAPACITY.
Keep a low profile, avoid risky places and vary your daily routine.

DO NOT TRY TO GO NATIVE.
Remember that you are assigned there to perform a function, and also that local people want to know you as an American.

REMEMBER THAT NORMAL VERSUS DEVIANT IS CULTURALLY DETERMINED.

EXPECT PROBLEMS AND MISTAKES, in spite of all preparations, **BUT AVOID CHALLENGING FUNDAMENTAL VALUES AND VIOLATING ESSENTIAL TABOOS.**

NOBODY IS PERFECT.

But we can all improve by learning about others and by adjusting ourselves.

BRING YOUR OWN CONTRIBUTION TO HUMAN UNDERSTANDING.

Raise the cultural pyramid farther up and share your discoveries with the rest of us, and the world of tomorrow will be better than today.

ENDNOTES

1. L. Robert Kohls, *Survival Kit for Overseas Living* (Yarmouth, ME: Intercultural Press Inc., 1984).
2. Based on Brent D. Ruben, "Human Communication and Cross-Cultural Effectiveness," in *International and Intercultural Communication Annual*, IV:1977, pp. 95-105.
3. Compiled by author from personal experience and various sources such as *Cross-Cultural Communication Course* (USAF Special Operations School, Hulbert Field, FL); Charles T. Vetter, Jr., *Citizen Ambassador* (Brigham Young University, David M. Kennedy International Center, 1983); and others.

General Bibliography

Almond, Gabriel A. and G. Bingham Powell Jr.
    1978 *Comparative Politics*. Boston: Little, Brown and Co., 1978.
Beaver, R. Pierce, ed.
    1982 *The World's Religions*. Grand Rapids, MI: Eerdmans Publishing Co., 1982.
Benedict, Ruth.
    1934 *Patterns of Culture*. Boston: Houghton Mifflin Co., 1934.
Condon, John C. and Fahti Yousef
    1977 *An Introduction to Intercultural Communication*. Indianapolis: Bobbs-Merrill Educational Publishing, 1977.
Deutsch, Karl W.
    1966 *Nationalism and Social Communication*. New York: McGraw-Hill, Inc., 1966.
Dodd, Carley H.
    1977 *Perspectives on Cross-Cultural Communication*. Dubuque, IA: Kendall/Hunt Publishing Company, 1977.
Fischer, Heinz-Dietrich and John C. Merrill, eds.
    1976 *International and Intercultural Communication*. New York: Hastings House Publishers, 1976.
Geertz, Clifford
    1973 *The Interpretation of Culture*. New York: Basic Books, Inc., Publishers, 1973.
Goldscheider, Calvin.
    1971 *Population, Modernization, and Social Structure*. Boston: Little, Brown and Co., 1971.
Haviland, William A.
    1983 *Cultural Anthropology*, New York: Holt, Rinehart and Winston, 1983.
Hesselgrave, David J.
    1978 *Communicating Christ Cross Culturally*. Grand Rapids, MI: Zondervan Publishing House, 1978.
Kohls, L. Robert
    1984 *Survival Kit for Overseas Living*. Yarmouth, ME: Intercultural Press, Inc., 1984.
Kraft, Charles H.
    1983 *Communication Theory*. Nashville: Abingdon Press, 1983.
Marsella, Anthony J., Roland J. Thorp and Thomas B. Ciborowski, eds.
    1979 *Perspectives of Cross-Cultural Psychology*. New York: Academic Press Inc., 1979.
Massey, Morris
    1979 *The People Puzzle*. Reston, VA: Reston Publishing Company, 1979.
McCrum, Robert
    1986 *The Story of English*. Dubuque, IA: Kendall/Hunt Publishing Company, 1986.
The Parker Pen Company
    1985 *Do's and Taboos Around the World*. Elmsford, NY: The Benjamin Company, Inc. 1985.
Rich, Andrea L.
    1974 *Interracial Communication*. New York: Harper and Row, Publishers, 1974.

Samovar, Larry A. and Richard E. Porter, eds.
    1976 *Intercultural Communication: A Reader*. Belmont, CA: Wadsworth Publishing Co., Inc., 1976.

Smith, Hedrick
    1976 *The Russians*. New York: Ballantine Books, 1976.

Stewart, Edward C.
    1974 *American Cultural Patterns: A Cross-Cultural Perspective*. Pittsburgh: University of Pittsburgh, 1974.

Vetter, Charles T.
    1983 *Citizen Ambassador*. Provo, UT: Brigham Young University, 1983.

Voslesensky, Michael
    1984 *Nomenklatura*. New York: Doubleday and Co., Inc., 1984.

Wrigley, E.A.
    1969 *Population and History*. London: Weidenfield and Nicholson, World University Library, 1969.